From This Day Forward

---

*First Lesson Sermons
For Lent/Easter
Cycle B*

Paul W. Kummer

CSS Publishing Company, Inc., Lima, Ohio

Scripture quotations are from the *Holy Bible, New International Version.* Copyright © 1973, 1978, 1984 International Bible Society. Used by permission of Zondervan Bible Publishers. All rights reserved.

Library of Congress Cataloging-in-Publication Data

Kummer, Paul W., 1963-
    From this day forward : first lesson sermons for Lent/Easter, cycle B / Paul W. Kummer.
        p.   cm.
    ISBN 0-7880-1379-3 (alk. paper)
    1. Lenten sermons. 2. Easter Sermons. 3. Sermons, American. 4. Catholic Church Sermons. 5. Bible Sermons. I. Title.
BV4277.K8   1999
252'.62—dc21   99-16012
                                                                                                          CIP

This book is available in the following formats, listed by ISBN:
        0-7880-1379-3   Book
        0-7880-1380-7   Disk
        0-7880-1381-5   Sermon Prep

For more information about CSS Publishing Company resources, visit our website at www.csspub.com.

*With gratitude to God for
my precious wife Susan,
who daily models the
faithfulness of his Son!*

Table Of Contents

Forsaking
All Others

Joel 2:1-2, 12-17

Can you see the young boys running through the city of Jerusalem yelling, "Blow the trumpets!" and the people of that city yelling back, "What?" "Blow the trumpets! Grab the shofar! We need to let everyone know!" And the people still scream back, "Why? What's going on?"

The adults know that the blowing of the trumpets in Jewish tradition can only mean one of three things: 1) It's time to move camp (but wait, we haven't lived in tents for decades!); 2) We need to get ready for war (but I didn't know there was even a potential conflict brewing!); or 3) The leaders are calling a sacred assembly (what could that be about?). The boys keep on shouting their alarm, stirring up the people.

Finally, the truth is learned. It's not only one of the reasons why the trumpets are traditionally blown, but a combination of two: war and the need to assemble. War with whom? Assemble to do what? The full impact of the alarm is understood when the verdict is announced by the prophet Joel, "God is at war with us and we must gather to repent!"

God is speaking through the Paul Revere of the ninth century B.C. as he warns his people that trouble is coming and they must repent. It's not a foreign army, but an army of locusts, and unless God relents all their crops will be destroyed and their livelihood devastated. Therefore, they must call a congregational meeting of humility and prayer to ask for God's mercy!

On this Ash Wednesday, God's prophets blow the trumpet in our hearing and sound the alarm: "Wake up! It's time to get serious

7

about sin. It's time to consecrate yourself to God." Like an alarm clock that goes off too early in the morning causing us to fight to obey its beckoning, so God yells to us in our slumber of sin, "It's time to change your ways!" But wait, we're good church-going people. We're even in attendance on this special Wednesday. We talk to God every day and ask for forgiveness, don't we? We even participate in the corporate Confession and Absolution each week in worship. Why another call for repentance?

God calls for repentance because too often we take it all for granted. If we're honest, we're too much like Private Daniels. His platoon readied for front-line action in the war and this young soldier seemed to come to a moment of truth. Turning to his close friend, he said, "Listen, Charlie, if I don't make it back and you do, would you take this letter and see that Sally gets it? Tell her my last thoughts were of her, and her name was the last word on my lips. And here's a letter for Jennifer. Tell her the same thing."

God is telling us to stop "two-timing" with the world, or three-timing with the world and Satan, or four-timing with the world, the devil, and our flesh, and be wholly dedicated to him! As we begin the Lenten season, we take the mask off, put our excuses down, and ask God to "search me and see if there be an offensive way in me." Any offensive way. No excuses. No hiding. Do surgery, God, and take out the cancer!

The Israelites had fought invading military forces before, but now they feared a more sinister threat: locusts (verses 3-11 provide a graphic description of their coming and destructiveness). The people could not resist them. Their army could not protect them. All they could do was depend on God. They had heard about the locusts their ancestors had seen in the exodus from Egypt. Now God was sending this sky-darkening, earth-destroying army on them? Why?

The Israelites had turned their backs on God. They had forgotten and forsaken him. They were involved with other girlfriends. Their heart beat for more than the one they married. How do we two-time God? By changing the language to make sin seem less harsh and rebellion more acceptable. We call lying merely "stretching the truth" and cheating "bending the rules a little." Adultery is trivialized to "having an affair" and murdering is "uncontrolled, but justified anger." What used to be called perversion is now called an "alternate lifestyle" and self-indulgence is now defined as "self-fulfillment." Impatient people are forgiven as only being "time conscious" and the divisive person is an "active defender of the truth." And what used to be murder of an unborn baby is now called "choice." No wonder God is upset. No wonder God demands that we change our ways. We can't be married to him and play the field at the same time! Sound the alarm! A day of darkness is at hand!

Who? Who is called to change their ways? Of course, the whole nation of Judah. But specifically look at who Joel says must humble themselves. First the elders, the respected older men of the communities, must lead by example, throw away sinful practices, and humble themselves before God. Then the children and even those still breastfeeding must admit sin and change. Hmmm. Yes, even children understand the concept of sin and telling God they're sorry. Babies are sinful too. The group of people listed next show how urgent this alarm is: even the man and woman who plan to kneel before God tomorrow and pledge their faithfulness must kneel before God *now* and put off their wedding plans. This is especially noteworthy when one knows that in the Old Testament newly married men were given a year off from military service to enjoy the union and nurture the new relationship. But not now! This call is more crucial than consummation. Finally, and most importantly, the priests (that's the pastors and leaders of the church) must become transparent before God and get rid of their sin! No one is left out. The alarm clock is blaring. Can everyone hear it?

Why? Why is this call for reflection and repentance so critical? Our text tells us that a "day of darkness and gloom" is at hand. The clouds and blackness will be so bad that the people of Israel are in danger of becoming a distant memory, a footnote in the history books. Their imminent destruction will cause the world to say, "Ah, look at their country now. And they thought they were so good!" The nation's once-greatness will be scorned and ridiculed! Worse yet, surrounding nations, at the sight of the disaster,

9

will ask a penetrating question: "What happened to their God? I thought he was more merciful and powerful than this!"

How? What is the way to avert this tragedy and win this war? Turn back to me, God says. Come with trembling bodies (v.1), broken hearts (v.13), and with weeping faces (v.17), crying out to the Lord for mercy! God calls for an external expression that mirrors an inside reality, yet he does not want only outward actions that are a façade for unrepentance inside. Too often our repentance, though perhaps begun with a genuine attitude of "I'm going to get all the junk out," turns into a "I'll give up the easy stuff and hold onto the junk I really like." We, in essence, are like the boy who was told repeatedly by his mom to sit down. The boy continued to stand, disobeying his mom. Finally, the mother went to him, and physically plopped him in a chair. Angry, the boy bellowed, "I may be sitting down on the *outside,* but I am standing on the *inside!*" Joel was preaching for a sincere change of heart which would show in brokenness and altered living.

What about us this holy Wednesday? Where is the "ring" of the alarm clock sounding in our country, in our congregation, in our individual hearts? Like the people of Judah, no one is left out. Children, where is God pricking your heart to stop fighting with Mom and Dad and to ask God to forgive you? With what nonchristian friends is he warning you not to go out to places that displease him? Adults, for what do you need to ask God for forgiveness and mercy? It might not be big in the world's eyes or compared to your neighbor's unfaithfulness, but neither are termites. But termites do silent, long-term destruction slowly. That's what happens when we push God out of one or more areas of our lives or try to hide fault from him. The sin might not be visible and immediately destructive, like a hurricane's vengeance, but God is still displeased. Married couples, those who recently or long ago were bride and groom, is God the center of your marriage in all areas? Could God walk through your home and look in your video cabinets or underneath the mattress and not be ashamed? Could he sit next to you as you watch television or surf the Web without being embarrassed? Sin is anything Jesus wouldn't do. And leaders of the church, are we "above reproach," fleeing from sin and "pursuing righteousness, godliness, faith, love, endurance, and gentleness" (1 Timothy 6:11)? It's not the other person who needs to look at God's mirror and see sin, but you!

Why is the call so urgent? Because everyone is looking at us as this century draws to a close to see what a Christian is really supposed to be. Have our acidic actions or verbal venom caused scorn to be brought upon the Body of Christ? Has our lack of love or exclusiveness made Jesus a byword? Do people see God for who he really is by what they see in you and me or are people mockingly saying, "If that's how God is, then I don't want any part!"

How does God expect us to react? I believe with trembling bodies, rent hearts, and tearstained faces. Do we ever ponder the greatness and holiness of God, and then consider our lowliness and unworthiness, so that we are almost shaken? If God were not merciful, we'd all shake with fear! What about our hearts? God says he will not despise a broken and contrite heart. Do our hearts break over our sin and the sin around us more than when our favorite team loses? What about tears? They don't have to be visible, but does our soul grieve for the lost in this world and for the way America has rejected God and lost her spiritual and moral moorings? God grieves! So should we! Are we sorry enough not only to ask God for forgiveness, but also never to do it again? Are we willing to get the junk out — all of it — even it it's difficult or we lose friends or it costs money?

The alarm has been sounded, but the trumpets only echo though the Judean hills now. What will be the outcome of a truly repentant heart, city, and country? *Forgiveness!* Can we be sure? *Yes!* God promises: "Return to the Lord your God, for he is gracious and compassionate, slow to anger and abounding in love, and he relents from sending calamity" (v.13)! What happens after the sin is confessed? It is wiped away by a more than merciful God who not only forgives, but also gives blessings abundant (v. 14). Why can we turn back? Because God already turned his back on Jesus on the Day of the Lord he experienced. When God turned the lights out in heaven on Good Friday 2,000 years ago, he was in effect turning his back and not only refusing to help his Son, but also rejecting him. Now God will never reject the one who returns to him and asks for mercy. When the church leaders and people mocked Jesus on the cross, they echoed Joel's words and said, "Where is your God?" God was nowhere. He'd left his Son to die. Now no one may ask that about you. God is your best friend, who will never leave.

A wayward son left home at age seventeen to make it on his own and get out from under the thumb of his dad. His parents only heard from him each Christmas. In time, after all the inheritance money the boy had received from his grandpa was spent and he realized how good he had had it at home, he called his mom and asked if it would be all right if he took a train home. He promised her he was off drugs and was done with licentious living. She was delighted, but he wanted her to check with his dad to make sure he'd accept him back.

The train tracks ran right behind his parents' property. There was a large oak tree near the trestle he had played on as a child. "Mom, if it's okay with Dad for me to come home, ask him to tie a white flag on that tree, and as I come by I'll know whether or not to get off at the next stop."

The boy was hungry for home. He was also nervous. Would his dad forgive him? Could he come home? When the train took the last curve before his home, he couldn't bear to look. He hurriedly asked his elderly seat partner to look and see if there was a white flag on the oak tree. The son closed his eyes and prayed.

Then he heard the man excitedly say, "Did you say *one* white flag, son? Why, every branch has a white flag attached to it!"

Oh, how mighty sin can be! But even more mighty is God's mercy! White flags of Jesus' righteousness fly for us. Our God says to us this Wednesday, "Return to me and I will return to you" (Malachi 3:7). We can change our hearts because God has shown us his heart!

The day of the Lord is today! This is his day to change us. You know that letter you have in your back pocket ready to give to Jennifer? Rip it up! You're a one-timer!

Arc Of The Covenant

Genesis 9:8-17

James Gilmour was a missionary to Mongolia and was asked to treat some wounded soldiers. He was not a doctor, but he did know how to give first aid. He dressed the wounds of two of the men, but the third had a badly broken thigh bone. Gilmour didn't know what to do, so he knelt by the man and prayed for help, knowing that God would answer.

As he pondered what to do next, a crowd of beggars came by asking for money. Though preoccupied with the wounded men, his heart went out to the needy paupers. Hurriedly, he gave them a few coins and some words of loving concern. A moment later he stared in amazement at one weary beggar who had remained behind. The starving man was little more than a living skeleton. The missionary suddenly realized that the Lord had brought him a walking lesson in human anatomy.

Gilmour asked the man if he might examine him. Carefully he traced his finger over the area corresponding to the wounded man and set the fracture. God had answered his prayer in an amazing way!

On Ash Wednesday we looked inside ourselves and pondered our unfaithfulness to God. Today we celebrate the faithfulness of God. Just as he was faithful to the request of missionary Gilmour, so God was faithful to another man many thousands of years ago. Our text is the familiar story of the morning after the deluge Noah and his family endured. God speaks to Noah and establishes a covenant with him and all his descendants and all life on the earth.

First, the past faithfulness of God is demonstrated in how he dealt with righteous Noah. If I were God, (it's a good thing I'm not!), I would not have saved even one family when the earth was so wicked and "every inclination of the thoughts of (man's) heart were only evil all the time" (Genesis 6:5). I would have very cleanly dispatched a plague that destroyed all the people on the earth and then started over. No one would have ever known. In fact, I would not have let the world regress as badly as it did — I would have started over immediately after Noah's predecessors ate the fruit which they were forbidden. Yet, God looked with mercy upon one family.

Second, God's present faithfulness is demonstrated in the agreement God made with Noah as he exited the ark. God required nothing from him or his descendants. God thought up the agreement, cut it with Noah, and declared it to be so. Yes, this man with great cabin fever had set up an altar, but only in thanks to his Creator for preserving his life. This was a one-sided covenant, a gift from the hand of a more-than-faithful God. Later on God's covenants required man's commitment to affirm something, do something, give something. Here God says, "I now establish my covenant with you and with your descendants after you and with every living creature that was with you" (v. 1).

Third, God's faithfulness is demonstrated in a promise. There will never be a worldwide flood again. And we know God has kept his word. There has never even been a whole country flood since Noah's day. Could God have flooded the whole earth? Yes, because he's that powerful. But no, because "God is not man that he should lie, nor a son of man, that he should change his mind. Does he speak and then not act? Does he promise and not fulfill?" (Numbers 23:19). Why did God promise and fulfill this promise? It is because God is merciful and faithful to James Gilmour, to Noah, and to you!

Felix of Nola was a Christian saint from the early church. Once, when persecution broke out, he had to flee from his enemies who wanted to kill him. As he fled he crawled into a cave to escape. As he prayed and lay in the darkness, spiders wove their webs across the narrow entrance. When his enemies came near, they noticed the webs and continued on, thinking he couldn't possibly be in there. Felix said, "When God isn't there, a wall is only like a spider's web. When God is there, a spider's web is like a wall!"

God not only spoke of his faithfulness, but also gave proof of what he promised. Like the spider's web of protection for Felix, the rainbow in the sky was assurance that God would take care of Noah and all his descendants. Imagine what Noah saw when they opened the door to the ark after more than a year on board. Dead creatures everywhere. Half carcasses used as food by flying animals. Total devastation and land formation shifts. Then they looked up. Mrs. Noah got out her camera to record it for posterity. The grandchildren ran to find the end of it and the pot of gold. One of Noah's sons began to write the meteorological manual on how a rainbow is formed. And Noah kept on shoveling manure, right? Are you kidding?

They'd never seen such a beautiful sight before. Imagine what memories, trepidation, and reflections on God's faithfulness went through their minds each time in the months and years to come when they saw another arc similar to the one that first encircled their ark. "O Lord, you don't just say it, you do it! You give signs and wonder to back up your word. You never fail." Talk about great family devotions with an object lesson included. "I have set my rainbow in the clouds and it will be the sign of the covenant between me and the earth."

God still gives us signs and wonders, marks of his covenant with us. The covenant he makes with us in baptism is a sign of his wonderful faithfulness to us. He even speaks of it in the context of the story of Noah. "God waited patiently in the days of Noah while the ark was being built. In it only a few people, eight in all, were saved through water, and this water symbolizes baptism that now saves you" (1 Peter 3:20-21). Just as the ark kept the family safe through the waters to the rainbow on the other side, so God takes his children through the waters of salvation to give them the ever-arching rainbow of the presence of the Holy Spirit. And the Spirit is more than an atmospheric phenomenon!

The other sign and wonder is not found under the sun and raindrops, but under the bread and wine. God's faithfulness is

15

demonstrated each time we partake of Holy Communion. What if God only *said* there would never be a global flood again? We can believe all he says, but the sign serves to reassure humankind even more. What if God only *said*, "Your sins are forgiven"? He means that, but he knows that human beings are programmed in such a way to need proof. So what did he do? He gave us tangible, physical evidence of his presence and power. Here's the way to think of it: What if your spouse pledged her love and faithfulness to you on your wedding day ten years ago. You have a good relationship, but she has not touched, caressed, or stroked you since the wedding night. She still says she loves you! Would you start to doubt her love? Of course. Probably nine years and eleven months and 29 days ago? God cherishes us continually like a newlywed. He touches and caresses us, his bride, in the holy meal so we have no doubt that he is for us! What a sign! How wonderful!

Baptism. Holy Communion. Noah's rainbow. All signs of God's faithfulness. What are some other rainbows that have been seen through the ages? The French philosopher Voltaire predicted that Christianity would be swept from existence within 100 years. Yet just fifty years after he died in 1779, the German Bible Society had occupied Voltaire's house and used his printing press to produce stacks of Bibles.

Another flood came during World War II when Adolf Hitler erected a massive stone structure in Monte Carlo to house a radio station from which to broadcast Nazi propaganda into North Africa. A rainbow shines today because from that very building, Trans World Radio beams the good news of Jesus' salvation all across Europe and into Russia and Africa!

I wonder if people really know today what a rainbow represents. It's not just light falling on a spray of water against a dark background, but a sign from God of his unending trustworthiness. The greatest proof of God's unending commitment to us is the rainbow in the form of a cross, high on a hill encircling all humankind. From Calvary shines forth God's everlasting covenant declaring, "I, the Lord, do not change" (Malachi 3:6) in the freedom from sin and death I offer to those who will come under the shadow of my rainbow and be washed in its blood red color! Just as God said to

Noah, "Whenever the rainbow appear in the clouds, I will see it and remember the everlasting covenant"(v. 16), so throughout this age God sees the cross with his Son nailed to it. That's how long his mercy shall prevail for sinners.

Until eternity we will be reminded of God's faithfulness and even then we will worship him around the throne for this faithfulness, for Revelation says, "At once I was in the Spirit, and there before me was a throne in heaven with someone sitting on it. And the one who sat there had the appearance of jasper and carnelian. A rainbow, resembling an emerald, encircled the throne" (Revelation 4:2-3).

The next time you see a rainbow be assured that the pot of gold at the end of it is God's eternal faithfulness!

A New Name

Genesis 17:1-7, 15-16

What names did people call you as you were growing up? What nicknames did your parents or grandparents saddle you with? I hope most of the names were endearing. But were others nasty or hurtful? Were you given a nickname because of how you looked or how you talked? Because of where you lived or what you wore?

Did anyone ever give you a name because they felt they knew what your future would hold? If so, did that spur you on in your destiny or did it hold you back and discourage you? Did they nick-name you in honor of what they believed you would become? I hope so!

On Ash Wednesday we were called to *change our ways*. Last week we were called to remember God's *unchanging ways*. Today we are called to celebrate our *name change*! First we needed to repent, and then we needed to be reminded of God's faithfulness, and today we are reminded of our purpose in life.

Lent is a call to renew our purpose for living on earth. Why did God choose us in the first place? Why did he work so hard through his Holy Spirit to change us? We could be spiritually opposed to God, but we're not. Why? Is it just so we can enjoy a pleasant life and as a result of our faith in Jesus go to an even better place someday? I don't think so.

It's because of a covenant, an agreement, God made with Abram centuries ago. This was another covenant of eternity even as Noah's was. In contrast to last week's covenant, however, this one is two-sided. God had already come to Abram and revealed his plan of action years earlier (chapter 15). In response to God's promises, Abram was walking with God (v. 1). Now he changes Abram's name and that of someone else very close to him. Then he put a specific call on Abram's life.

I wonder what nicknames Abram had in school or on the soccer field before God got a hold of him. Perhaps he was called Abe or Ram. When God began his work, he lengthened Abram's given name because he was in the process of changing his purpose for living. "Abram" had an impressive meaning already: "lofty father." Others might have been pleased, but not Abram, because he wasn't even a father yet, much less feeling lofty. So when God changed his name to Abraham, which means "father of many," Abe had a choice: either see it as a cruel joke or see it as a name given in faith by a big God who could yet bring sons from his body. God always gives names that declare what he has done, even if it is only by faith at the time. The name change also put a call on Abram's life: to be "very fruitful; I will make nations of you, and kings will come from you" (v. 6). The entire Jewish nation has come from Abraham; the King of kings came from the ancestry of this man and all the Church too!

What nicknames did Abram's wife endure growing up? What pet names did Abram have for Sarai? There was someone who loved Sarai even more than Abram did, and he changed her name, too. From a beautiful moniker meaning "princess" or "the heroine" (both complimentary in their own right), God changed her name to Sarah, because he had planned something magnificent for her. She would be destined "to rule," "to overcome," and to "triumph" as a princess over what? Her infertility. And she did. All Jewish mamas are descendants of Sarah. Her call was to be the "mother of nations," and "kings of people will come from her" (v. 16). Indeed they did! What a calling!

God delights in changing people's lives and their names, too. Think of all the examples in the Bible where God graciously effected a change of heart, then changed the given name on the birth certificate. Jacob, for example (Genesis 32), after an all night wrestling match with God, was given the name Israel to represent the struggle he had just endured. It also characterized Jacob's coming boldness to serve the God of his fathers and predicted the struggles and victories to come of the people named after him, the children of Israel.

We know of a man named Saul who didn't always go by that name. Though it wasn't changed immediately after God miraculously turned Saul around, Saul, which means "asked of God," became Paul, which means "little." Because of the greatness of Paul's ministry, perhaps God wanted Paul to remember where his "bigness" and power came from, so that he could be even more effective in God's kingdom.

And, of course, as God was changing Peter's life to one of stability and less frequent eruption, Jesus gave Peter a name in faith of who he would become! Peter means "a pebble," but he was renamed "Rock." No longer would he be just a stone in someone's shoe, but a force to be reckoned with, a large, noticeable boulder built on the foundation of Christ the solid rock. As one of the chief apostles who established the Church, Peter lived up to the billing.

What about you and me during this Lenten season? If God were to show up at your coffee break room at work or the locker room at the club or listen to your conversation on the phone, what nicknames would he hear you being called? How has God changed your life so that you have a different name, a different outlook, and a new future?

If you are a believer in Christ (thus a descendant of Abraham) and one who depends on Jesus alone for salvation, you have already been given a new name. When you were baptized — or whenever your faith birthday was — your middle name was changed to "Christian." Scott Christian Miller. Susan Christian Wise. Even if you are named after a grandparent or parent, your given middle name is not nearly as important as the Christ at the center of your life. Another name that God has given us is "saint." Wait. Isn't that reserved for people with white hair, for people in heaven already, or for people of the stature of the late Mother Teresa? No, you have the nickname of "saint" because you are a holy one, made holy through the blood of Jesus. Jesus, through the prophet Isaiah, hundreds of years before he was even born said to you,

"Fear not, for I have redeemed you; I have summoned you by name; you are mine" (43:1).

There is a story about two young brothers who were caught stealing sheep. The punishment back then was to brand the thief's forehead with the letters *S.T.*, which stood for sheep thief. One brother subsequently left the village and spent his remaining years wandering from place to place indelibly marked by disgrace. The other remained in the village, made restitution for the stolen sheep, and became a caring friend and neighbor to the townspeople — an old man loved by all.

Many years later, a stranger came to town and inquired about the *S.T.* on the old man's forehead. "I'm not sure what it means," another told him. "It happened so long ago, but I think the letters must stand for *saint*."

God has a myriad of other names to describe his beloved children, but his favorites are names that describe a person who fulfills his purpose after he gets a name change.

During World War II, a church in Strasbourg, France, was destroyed. Little remained but rubble. When that was cleared, a statue of Christ, standing erect, was found. It was unbroken except for the two hands, which were missing.

In time, the church was rebuilt. A sculptor, noticing the missing hands on the statue of Christ, said, "Let me carve a new statue of Christ, with hands." Church officials met to consider the sculptor's proposal. His offer was rejected. A spokesman for the church said, "Our broken statue will serve to remind us that Christ touches the hearts of men, but he has not a hand to minister to the needy or feed the hungry or enrich the poor except our hands."

That's the calling Christians (little Christs) and saints have on their lives: to be the hands and feet of Jesus in this world. It's the same calling that Abraham and Sarah had and it is why God called Jacob, Saul, and Peter by new names: to point to the cross of Jesus. It's a calling to declare with Paul and Peter that there is no other name by which we must be saved and have abundant life now.

How well are we living up to the name God gave us: Christian? Alexander the Great was reviewing his troops as they prepared for war. As he walked along the straight lines, he found one disheveled soldier. Standing directly in front of the soldier, he barked at him and said, 'What is your name, private? "Alexander, sir!" came the reply. Staring even more sternly at him, the Emperor asked again, "What is your name?" Again the soldier said, "Alexander, sir!" Without hesitation, the Commander in Chief once again asked him, "Private, I said, what is your name?" Bewildered, the soldier meekly said, "Alexander, sir!" The leader then replied, "Well, private, either change your conduct or change your name!" The Holy Spirit is the one who "works in you to will and to act according to his good purposes" (Philippians 2:13). He makes and keeps us as little Christs.

As we walk with Christ and carry his name, how well are we doing at fulfilling our mission? Every Christian has a call on his/her life to make an eternal spiritual difference in the world each day. I pray that for myself each day. Even as Abraham and Sarah were called to be very fruitful and be the father and mother of kings, so we are too!

I know someone who views the parable of the seeds sown upon different soils in the New Testament as a challenge to Christians to pray for fruit and harvests in our lives. But he pleads, "Don't settle for thirty or sixty times what was sown, but at least 100 times the fruit." In fact, he prays specifically that God will not take him home until he's allowed to influence thousands of people for Christ. "Lord, don't let me die until at your throne I can rejoice that you saved and nurtured 5,000 precious souls through me!" Many nations, Lord. I want to be very fruitful. We all know we can't take anything to heaven. Except people.

Do we think long term in this mission or just about our neighbor or cubicle partner whom we want to fall in love with Christ? Do we think about our descendants coming after us? When God made his covenant with Abraham, he had a long-term perspective in mind. You will affect generations to come, Abe, so that I can be "the God of your descendants after you" (v. 7). What about the children you are nurturing right now in your home? Or the children you are teaching in Sunday School? Or your grandchildren or the children you have adopted in the neighborhood? You are being called and used by God to cultivate "kings of people" for the kingdom of God. Your physical children or your spiritual children can become mighty warriors for Jesus through your influence and they, in turn, might change a nation or people group. It's never too late to take this calling seriously. Abraham was 99 years old and Sarah ninety when the beginning of this promise and covenant came to fruition.

Francis of Assisi once invited a young monk to join him on a trip to town to preach. Honored to be asked, the monk gladly accepted. All day long he and Francis walked through the streets, alleyways, the byways, and even the suburbs. They saw and interacted with hundreds of people. At day's end, the two headed back home. Not even once had Francis addressed a crowd, nor had he specifically talked to anyone about Jesus. His young companion was deeply disappointed and confused. "I thought we were going into town to preach." Francis replied, "My son, we *have* preached. We were preaching while we were walking. We were seen by many and our behavior was closely watched. It is of no use to walk anywhere to preach unless we preach everywhere as we walk!" We have a life-long, life-changing, lifestyle calling because we have a new name given to us by God himself.

No nickname or title you bear is as important as the name God has given you. And no one can take it away. As you give your children nicknames, I urge you to make them ones which, first of all, remind them of their status with Christ. Second of all, use the nickname as a means of giving them a sense of destiny and encouragement as they fulfill their calling as a Christian. Why? So they may also be very fruitful in the generations to come.

An anonymous author has penned these words which aptly describe our purpose for living:

> *You are writing a gospel, a chapter each day,*
> *By deeds that you do, by the words that you say;*
> *People read what you write, whether faithless or true —*
> *Say, what is the gospel according to you?*

Our Jealous Husband

Exodus 20:1-17

These are Ten Commandments that little children know to be true:

1. When your mom is mad at your dad, don't let her brush your hair.
2. No matter how hard you try, you can't baptize cats.
3. You can't trust dogs to watch your food.
4. Never hold a dustbuster and a cat at the same time.
5. You can't hide a piece of broccoli in a glass of milk.
6. Puppies still have bad breath even after eating a tic-tac.
7. When your sister hits you, don't hit her back. They always catch the second person.
8. Don't sneeze when someone is cutting your hair.
9. Reading what people write on desks can teach you a lot.
10. The best place to be when you are sad is in Grandma's lap.

I wonder if the same children know the Ten Commandments that delineate more important issues than wise words about cats and dogs and sisters. Does anyone know and believe in the Ten Commandments from the finger of God anymore?

The first commandment read earlier was "When your mom is mad at your dad, don't let her brush your hair." What is the first commandment from the Almighty? "You shall have no other gods before me." Get God in place first in your life — and everything else will fall into place.

Think of it this way: When you get dressed in the morning and you must button up a shirt, a skirt, or a jacket, do you start from the bottom or the top? Which button do you fasten first? Of course, the top one. But — have your ever had the frustrating and time-consuming tragedy occur when you thought you had it lined up, but after you buttoned up all the buttons, you discovered that you were still one off? You have to undo them all and then start over again. If you don't get the first button right, all else is out of alignment.

Or think of the last time you broke open your piggy bank and rolled the coins to take to the bank. If you didn't get that first coin straight in the bottom of the wrap, the subsequent 49 pennies didn't fit. When you've helped stack chairs at church on a movable rack, have you ever had the misfortune of lining up several chairs but then finding out they are sliding backwards because some dummy didn't place the inaugural one in correctly? Now the rack is all messed up.

That's how God feels about the Ten Commandments. The first one is the pinnacle of all and must be obeyed if the other nine are to be in alignment. No other gods. No one before the true God. Don't have any love or allegiance in front of your Creator. In other words, love God with all your heart, soul, mind, and strength — with all you've got! — because he deserves it. No one else does! If we could get that button secured first and always, the rest of the buttons are much easier to fasten.

But are we willing to admit that we don't know how to stack chairs very well? That we have trouble rolling coins? A young man once lived in a small community. He was known for his extreme pride. One day, he walked into the village blacksmith shop shortly after the blacksmith had thrown a horseshoe on the ground to cool. Seeing it here, the young man reached down, picked it up, but instantly cast it aside as it burned his fingers.

"Kind of hot, isn't it, son?" said the blacksmith. "No, it's not hot," said the prideful young man. "It just doesn't take me long to look at a horseshoe!" Pride can be a god in itself, thus making it even harder to get the first commandment right.

God is calling his people to keep the main thing the main thing: Love for and allegiance to him above all else. This Lenten season is a good time to reflect how many other gods we are allowing to infect and afflict our lives. The rest of the commandments form the basis for this nine-step examination:

Who is the god of your worship? When you pray or sing to God or when you join in corporate worship in a sanctuary or when you read your Bible alone, is your god God or are your thoughts, "I had better do this so God will bless me. I'll get this over so I can move on to more important things. I'll put in my time so I can say I did so!" Your god in worship, in that case, is yourself. You are more concerned about how good you'll look or what you can get from God. Oops, that button is out of place!

Who is the god of your tongue? "Don't misuse God's name." When we use the Divine names as expletives or to deceive someone with emphasis, we surely do something God wouldn't do with his own names. Who's behind the mud being slung at the character of Jesus? Ah, it's the one who wishes he was God and got kicked out of heaven because of that damning desire. Oh, God, heal my tongue!

Who is the god of your weekend? Gods like attention; in fact, the true One deserves it. What gets most of your attention on the weekend? The television? Your children? Your bed? Your friends? The fishing pole? That elusive white ball? Your yard? Where does button number one fit in time-wise on your weekends? Is it Pastor Sheets and Deacon Pillow with whom you spend time or the people and pastor at your church? Do you give Jehovah the attention he deserves?

Who is the god of your submission? "I don't answer to anyone but God," you might say, but then your mistaken notion of what this commandment means is your god. God is he to whom we ultimately bow as authority, but he's given us the government and parents, policemen and teachers to whom we must submit. God has placed them over us. And for whom does God command us to pray: all leaders and those in authority.

Well, pastor, so far so good for me! I genuinely worship God most of the time. God has 97 percent control of my tongue. I never miss church unless I'm sick. And I respect authority (unless I'm real late to a meeting, then I turn on my fuzz-buster). Be careful, dear Christian, in calculating how "good" you are. That can cause the first chair to slide on that cart. Besides, the only person you should compare yourself to is the One who never broke a single commandment.

In the Old West, Buck was known as the "meanest man in the territory." He robbed banks, raped, and murdered — right up to the end. His brother Ned, with whom he shared the loot, nevertheless offered 10,000 dollars to any preacher who would conduct Buck's funeral and call him a "saint." One preacher, eyeing the reward, agreed to do so. In his funeral sermon, he said to the living brother, "God will judge the deceased, but with stolen silver you want to buy a favorable verdict from God. *Compared to you*, Ned, your brother was a saint!"

Who is the god of your anger? Jesus said that if you are even angry with your brother, you are guilty of murder. Yes, there is such a thing as righteous anger, but that's the kind that God would have toward the offending party. Are you sure God is mad at what disgusts you or are you being your own god?

Who is the god of your sexuality? Is the freedom (actually bondage!) god of the '60s or the "feel good" god of popular society or the "I can't help it, god!" of our flesh what controls your thoughts and actions. Sex was God's idea. He thinks it's wonderful — as long as he's in charge!

Who is the god of your possessions? Which god, God or Satan, wins the battle each time you file your taxes and you try to squeeze that extra amount in for a deduction? Which god, God or the world, is victorious when the Ramada Inn towels are large and cushy? Which god, God or your flesh, controls you when your neighbor doesn't specifically request back the tool you borrowed a year ago? Oops, looks like you won't fit all those pennies in that roll!

A thief in New Jersey stole 7,000 dollars in jewelry, old coins, and cash from a widow. The items taken were all she had left from her husband's estate. In sorting through his loot, the thief came across several church envelopes containing money the woman intended to give to the Lord. Leaving their contents inside, he put them in another envelope, addressed it to the woman's church, and then dropped it in the mail. Hmmm. It's okay to steal from a widow, but not from the church? How morally confused our world is!

Who is the god of your relationships? Are you like God in forgiving those who hurt you or do you have your own standard? God says, "I have loved you with an everlasting love!" Is our love never lasting? Jesus never opened his mouth when accused ... oh, forget it, we won't go there.

Who is the god of your desires? Someone gets a new car. Is your reaction, "Nice car. I'm glad God blessed you with it," or, "Nice car! Why didn't God give me one too?" Godliness with contentment is great gain. How much gain we get is directly related to who is god of our desires. Darn, those button holes never line up!

Can you imagine anyone ever getting the first commandment right and then perfectly keeping the rest? Wouldn't you like to meet that person? You can. You have. He lives inside your heart, dear Christian. Imagine, Jesus never disobeyed his parents. He never lusted after things or a woman. He didn't just happen to forget to return a library book. He never called anyone a "jerk" unrighteously!

What is more amazing is that though he never sinned, God understands our weakness and wants to help us get everything buttoned up right. If we'll only ask, he'll empower us. But we're afraid to go to him. Why?

A woman was driving home alone one evening when she noticed a man in a truck following her. Growing increasingly fearful, she exited the freeway and headed for a well-lit gas station. The truck stayed with her, even running the red light to do so.

In a panic, the woman wheeled into the station, jumped from her car, and ran inside screaming. The truck driver ran to her car, jerked the back door open, and pulled from the floor behind her seat a man who was hiding there.

The lady was fleeing from the wrong person. She was running from the one who could save her. The truck driver, seated high enough to see her back seat, had spied the would-be rapist and was pursuing her to save her, even at his own peril.

During this Lenten Season, when we can get overwhelmed with our sinful condition, let's not forget to run to the One who saves us from the other gods in our lives. They cannot help us; they only want to destroy what God has already begun in our lives. Our jealous God wants us all for himself and will not only forgive us for having other gods, but also give us the desire and the ability to keep the chair cart and the coin holder straight.

Jesus' death and resurrection give us brand new clothes of righteousness and those buttons are always fastened properly!

Just What The Doctor Ordered

Numbers 21:4-9

A wealthy entrepreneur was consternated to find a fisherman sitting lazily beside his boat. "Why aren't you out there fishing?" he asked.

"Because I've caught enough fish for today," said the fisherman.

"Why not catch more than you need?" the rich man asked.

"What would I do with them?"

"You could earn more money," came the impatient reply, "and buy a bigger boat so you could go deeper and catch more fish. You could purchase nylon nets, catch even more fish, and make more money. Soon you'd have a fleet of boats and be rich like me."

"Then what would I do?" the fisherman asked.

"You could sit down and enjoy life," said the tycoon.

"What do you think I'm doing right now?" the fisherman replied as he looked contentedly at the sea.

In today's text, the people of Israel play the role of the rich tycoon and God wanted them to be like the contented fisherman. The people of Israel would have killed for some fish to eat in the middle of the desert as they wandered, but all they had was an attitude: "We detest this miserable food" (v.5)! It was manna, heavenly food, angel's food, but they were tired of it. Some scholars say that the word "manna" came from the word meaning, "to despise," so that the very name of the daily provision from the hand of God was being mocked every time they gathered it in the morning.

The Israelites are not any different from us, and I believe God teaches us a three-part lesson through this experience of the children

31

of Israel: first, their impatience (vv. 4-6); second, their petition. (vv. 6-7); third, God's prescription (vv. 8-9).

Impatience

Here is a list of all the miracles, saving actions, provisions, and general people-keeping that God had done for his people in the recent years before this story:

- Enemies routed by spectacular means
- An invisible tour leader of fire and cloud
- Ten devastating displays, "but none came near their house"
- A path through water that shouldn't have been there
- Instead of a faucet, they just "turned on" a rock
- Fire and smoke and quaking on Mount Sinai

God had given them protection, provisions, leadership, and day by day wisdom, yet they forgot all his goodness and could only see the hard side of life. What short memories they had of times when God bailed them out and of how much better life was when they followed him. Were they really starving or dying of thirst? There was food; it was just not the kind they liked and they were tired of the "worthless stuff."

They remind me of the grandma who took her grandson to the beach on a windy day. As she lay in the sun getting a tan, her grandson wandered away unnoticed. She only knew of his where-abouts when she heard him screaming for help in the surf. He had wandered too far into the water and was in danger of being swept away by the tide.

Immediately Grandma started to pray, "O God, help my grand-son!" No one else heard his cries and she couldn't swim, so she was helpless to do anything. She could only pray. Moments later a big wave simply lifted her grandson safely onto shore. She ran to him, held and comforted him, but instead of thanking God, she looked toward heaven and said, "Where's his hat? He had a hat when he went out there."

What about us? Impatience before God is not something we often think of as a sin. Discontentment, despite his good gifts, indeed is an offense against God. No, it's not as visible as other sins, but how often do we get an attitude about the way life is dealt us or look up toward heaven and complain about the "food" God has sent us?

The "food" could be physical provisions. (Lord, why can't we have more "stuff" like our friends?) Or it could be how your family gets along. (Do something, God, with my sister!) We might struggle with thanking God for our daily emotional strength or our position at work. (It could be better, Lord!) We forget about all the good gifts he has lavished on us — because we want more!

The area where many people struggle is contentment in the moment — enjoying what one is doing and is blessed with now, instead of always looking for something in the future. In my house one would have heard this conversation frequently at night between my wife and me as we lay in bed, until I realized what I was doing.

> Me: I'm tired. I can't believe the day is over already.
>
> Susan: It's been a good day. Let's pray and go to sleep.
>
> Me: I wish I had more time in the day. I wish I would've had time to work in the yard. I hope tomorrow I get more done.
>
> Susan: No wishing, Paul. You can't change today or control tomorrow. God has all your times in his hands.
>
> Me: Yeah, but I wish we could just escape, get away.
>
> Susan: Sweetheart, let's just enjoy this moment and thank God for what he did do through us today.

Who are we really speaking against when we complain? Not our spouse, but God who gave her to us. Not the government, but the Leader who enthrones all leaders. Not our house, but the One who provided us with a place to live. We are complaining against God Almighty — if we believe he is still in control.

Petition

The Lord didn't take kindly to the people's complaining, and he sent snakes to punish the people. Like the grandma, Moses prayed on behalf of the people. He interceded for them when they asked. It's a good thing Moses was there to stand between them and God or else the whole nation might have been wiped out. His petition for mercy from God was all the people had.

This wasn't the first time Moses interceded for the people. Moses knew that role well. Obviously, Moses had been their representative to Pharaoh to get them out of their slavery in Egypt. He was the go-between at Mount Sinai when he received the law the people were to live by. And at least one other time, Moses saved the people from certain destruction when God's anger burned against them after they worshiped the golden calf. "But Moses sought the favor of the Lord his God. 'O Lord,' he said, 'why should your anger burn against your people, whom you brought out of Egypt with great power and a mighty hand?' " (Exodus 32:11). Moses was definitely a petitioning prophet!

There are other examples in the Bible of people who intervened for others who were displeasing to God. Job did it for his "friends" at God's request and God said, "I will accept his prayer and not deal with you according to your folly" (42:8). Paul wrote to the new Christians at Rome with such "great sorrow and unceasing anguish" that he would be willing to be cut off from the covenant with God if that would help save more of his countrymen who were dying in their sins. And Jesus himself intercedes before the throne of his Father as a result of his perfect going-between for us as epitomized in his cry from the cross, "Father, forgive them, for they know not what they are doing!"

Perhaps the cure for impatience is to petition. What better time is spent than praying for others when we feel cheated? What better attitude can we have than praying for others in the midst of an encroaching disgruntled spirit!

Prescription

Aren't you glad that God doesn't punish the sin of discontentment and bellyaching today the same way he did in Moses' day? Would any of us be alive? But the answer, the medicine, the healing balm — the prescription — is still the same: something lifted up.

When Moses petitioned God, God heard. But he asked Moses to do a strange thing: make a cast in the form of a snake, fill it with liquid metal and fashion a bronze snake. Huh? Then God said something even more strange, "Have the people look up at the snake attached to a pole and they will not die." Wow! I wonder if Moses hesitated at all.

Why a snake? Perhaps because it represented the death of a snake and therefore the substitute for a man so that he could live. Perhaps the bronze, reddish color would be a foreshadowing of Christ's atonement and purification through blood.

Why were they required to look at it? It took faith to believe that acknowledging the presence and power of something lifted up could take away the death threat clinging to their legs. I'm sure some of the Israelites thought it was stupid. They also died. Others probably remembered the blood on the doorpost to which they looked for salvation many years earlier and listened to God's servant Moses once again.

The prescription is still the same. From the time a snake first caused sin in Eden because of an unspoken complaint by Eve to the bronze snake on a pole at Moses' time to the time Jesus crushed the serpent's head at Calvary and beyond, the medicine is a substitute and faith.

The deadly poison of sin has existed in man since the Fall. The bronze serpent had no poison in it. So also when the perfect Jesus was lifted up on the cross in the likeness of sinful flesh, he took our place. He took our poison. He endured the punishment we deserve for our incessant impatience and grumbling. All God asks is that we look with faith to that pole of Calvary to see our freedom there. Some people think we're stupid for trusting in the power of the cross. No, it doesn't make sense. But it does save. God can't and won't punish us as Christians, even though we complain, because his Son already endured that penalty. He crushed the conniving snake once for all. We need not fear the devil.

Jesus saw this story as so significant for our spiritual life that it is the only Old Testament picture he applied to himself. The snake on a tree foreshadowed himself nailed to the cross: "But I, when I am lifted up from the earth, will draw all men to myself" (John 12: 32).

This account is the last recorded complaint of the wandering Israelites. Perhaps they learned much from this event. Have you?

You don't have a big boat? You've never caught your limit of fish? Everyone else seems to have more than you do? Your hat was lost at sea? You never even knew your grandma? You feel like life is one monotonous day after another?

Let this still your disquieted heart: someone is praying for you that you might have all that you need. And he also has the desire to give it to you! And that same Someone, who owned the whole world but gave it all up, was lifted up for you that you might know that he loves you.

Something Old, Something New

Jeremiah 31:31-34

It's amazing how fast things change. I can remember when I was a teenager how excited I was to purchase a used 8-track tape player to play my favorite music. No sooner had I reveled in that than I needed a cassette recorder to enjoy the newest artists because everything was changing to that format. Today tapes seem so noisy and cumbersome compared to the compact discs that are available. And I know there is newer technology out there that will someday replace my nicely stacked CDs. And all this while two crates of record albums are getting warped in the attic. My, how things change.

And though I am a novice on the computer compared to most people, even I have chronicled in my mind the changes the last few years. I can listen to my CDs through the computer. The computer now tells you when your grammar is bad and even suggests changes. I can not only e-mail someone and "talk" to him and receive a message from him simultaneously, but with the correct equipment, I can also see him across the miles while I type on the keyboard. What other new things will increase my incredulity even more tomorrow?

God is into new things too! Not music or computers, but new relationships with people.

But wait! Why something new? What's wrong with the LPs and the room-size computers? They don't work anymore. Nor does the old relationship. That relationship with God "broke" just like a scratched, dusty Frank Sinatra album, and it has become obsolete like the parts and pieces of computers that end up in the city dump every day. Why?

" 'Because they broke my covenant, though I was a husband to them,' declares the Lord."

So many people come to pastors in today's world (thank God they do come to us and not always directly to the lawyer) and tell us they have lost their love for their spouse. "I just don't love him anymore!" "I don't see any way out except divorce if I'm ever going to be happy again!" "We just need to start afresh and get on with our lives separately!" The record was broken and the computer crashed for good!

Now imagine that one of these spurned husbands whose wife has been admittedly unfaithful numerous times comes back to the pastor after the divorce settlement and says, "Forget it." Not forget her, but forget all that sin and pain; I want her back. If she is willing to start fresh — together — I want to remarry her. We want you to perform the reconciliation ceremony and write up a new marriage certificate. We'll redo our vows and re-pledge our faithfulness. All is forgiven and in the past.

That's hard to imagine in this "tit-for-tat" world of hard hearts and unforgiveness. But it happens. And it happened in the relationship between the children of Israel and their husband, God! He created a new covenant (marriage commitment) with them, and we are a part of that new covenant today. Why was there the need for a new marriage? Not because God didn't keep his wedding vows, but because his bride was continually unfaithful to God. The Old Testament community loved other men constantly more than her childhood sweetheart and that broke God's heart. The covenant with Noah wasn't enough for the wayward wife. Abraham's covenant wasn't honored for very long. The other covenants were ignored after a while and the people of Israel didn't even go to a lawyer. They just deserted their first love. This was the only marriage in trouble that didn't have two sides to the story. God was totally innocent; the people defiantly guilty.

Yet God wouldn't give up. He didn't find another wife. He just kept wooing the adulterous one. His love and commitment finally convinced his wife to come back and repledge her faithfulness. God made a new covenant with Israel.

What was new about this agreement? "I will put my law in their minds and write it on their hearts. I will be their God and they will be my people" (v. 33). The newness was that no longer would God let her out of his sight, but would forever be with her so she couldn't stray. She'd never be alone to be tempted and his love and adoration of her would always be her companion. In other words, he would live inside her and empower her. God did that when he sent Jesus not only to be one of us, but to reside in us by his Holy Spirit! That's what the Holy Spirit's desire and job is.

No longer did the Children of Israel need the Ark of the Covenant, which held the tablets of God's law, because that law had no power to help the people obey. But the Spirit within us not only tells us what is right and wrong, but also gives us the ability to choose right! No longer is the law inscribed in stone, but on every heart that knows Jesus! We don't hear only prophets' stark words but have our minds set on things above. Our love for God is an impulse and inspiration from within, not something difficult to follow like an external dictator. No, he is our friend!

Why did God promise this and then fulfill it with Jesus and his Spirit? Because God is patient. Another word is long-suffering. He "suffers long" in our unfaithfulness and our looking for love in all the wrong places. He cherishes his creation even though they spurn him. He never lost his love — either his feelings of love or his commitment to love us. How different from us!

God not only says he still loves us and wants us, but proves it by doing what only he can do: forgiving and wiping away our sins and not remembering them anymore (v. 34). He suffers long and his memory is short. When we confess our sins to God and repent of them, he "treads our sins underfoot and hurls all our iniquities into the depths of the sea" (Micah 7:19). We're the ones that remember them. The day after we bare our soul to God in confession, we often say to him, "Lord, remember that sin I confessed yesterday that I felt so bad about? Well, I still feel bad." What does God say back? "What sin? I've forgotten it all. It's buried and gone. Don't you remember it either!"

God's not like us or the businessman who was famous for saving everything (and we're not talking about computers). His file drawers were bulging. One day his exasperated secretary asked if she could dispose of all the old, useless material. The boss hesitated, but she was insistent. "All right," he finally agreed, "but be sure to make a copy of everything before you throw it away!"

God remembers his covenants and all the promises he makes. He remembers what the rainbow stands for. He knows and remembers your name. He counts and remembers the number of hairs on your head. He "remembers that we are dust" (Psalm 103:14). Because he is God his memory compares to no one else. He won't forget the anniversary when you were married to him in faith. He doesn't forget any of the good things you do for him. He won't forget how many trials and trouble you can handle. Does God forget anything? Yes, God has Alzheimer's in one area: our sins.

Are there any marriages here today which could use a new infusion of long-suffering and short memories? Who here need to be more like God to their spouse either in patience or in forgiveness? You might be in a horrible marriage of unfaithfulness and pain. God's been through it with his people and he loves to provide new relationships.

A Zulu chieftain's wife was converted at a missionary revival in Africa. She came home a changed person but her husband didn't like it. He told her he'd kill her if she ever went back to the missionary compound.

The new Christian wife didn't know what to do. She wanted to obey God as well as she could. She chose to visit with the missionaries again. When her husband found out that she had disobeyed him, he beat her so savagely that she lost her vision and the use of one arm completely. He left her on the path to the missionaries' house for the night.

In the morning, he felt remorseful enough to look for her. He found her where he had dragged her the night before. "What's your Jesus going to do for you now?" he scorned.

His wife said weakly, "He's going to help me forgive you."

God's mercies for all relationships here on earth and with him are new every morning. And that surely beats any upgrade on Windows 98.

Shameless Passion

Isaiah 50:4-9a

Today is Palm Sunday. Some of you wonder why our text is not highlighting the trek into Jerusalem on a donkey, but rather this coming Friday's story of Jesus' suffering as found prophesied in the Old Testament. Why is this the chosen lesson?

Too many people move from Palm Sunday's jubilation to Easter's victory and never take the excruciating walk through the Upper Room, the Garden of Gethsemane, the Trials, and Mount Calvary. But you must go through it all really to know the joy of the Open Tomb!

I like the other name chosen for this day: Passion Sunday. Yes, "passion" means "suffering" on our church calendar. This is called Passion Week. We thank Jesus for enduring his passion and pain for us. But can we not also, just for the next few minutes, read this text and see the dictionary definition of "passion" in Jesus too? The definition of passion is "that for which one feels a strong desire or liking."

You know a lot of people who are very passionate about certain things. Golf is the passion of many men and women. They spend lots of money to belong to a club, spend a whole morning chasing a little white ball, twist a club after a bad shot, spend more money in the club's restaurant afterwards, and then go home and watch golf on television. I'd say they are passionate about golf.

Other people are passionate about collecting things. Like pigs. I know a woman who has been collecting pigs — all different sizes and shapes. She has potholder pigs, ornamental pigs, letter opener pigs, flower vase pigs, socks with pigs on them, tongs with a pig head on it, pig wrapping paper, pig napkins, pig air fresheners. All she ever gets for Christmas and birthday gifts are piggish things. She's still passionate about pigs.

My wife is the most passionate person I have ever met. We've been married less than two years, but besides her passion for our marriage, she is passionate about life in general — always going full bore into everything. She'll lose herself in her piano playing or cooking or playing a game — and forget all about the time. Until I spoil the fun and bring her back to reality. She gives her all to be everything to everyone! That's passion!

Jesus was passionate too. Our text delineates three areas in his life: 1) passion to hear and listen to his Father (v. 1); 2) passion to give his life willingly (v. 6); 3) passion not to be disgraced nor let his children be shamed (v. 7-9).

Let's look at these three longings of Jesus and hear God speak to us.

He Heard And Listened To His Father

The only reason Jesus could be passionate about his mission and ministry, even though he only had three years to do it all and, as God, knew what the end would be, is because he was in tune with his Father. His Father wakened him "morning by morning" so he could be taught. Jesus took time to listen. We know the numerous times Jesus got up early in the morning and went to "lonely places" to pray and communed with his source of strength and wisdom — his daddy.

Isn't it interesting that the One who opened mouths and ears with wet mud and a word is the same one who opened his ears to hear from God? God listening to God. The all-knowing One being taught. Is that not a model for us to follow, we who think we're so smart? Jesus did have "an instructed tongue," because he never said or did anything without direction from his father. "I do nothing on my own but speak just what the Father has taught me. The one who sent me is with me; he has not left me alone, for I always do what pleases him" (John 8:28-29).

Jesus both heard and spoke words that "sustain the weary." What are these weary sustaining words for us today as we listen to him? Listen to your Daddy saying, "Come to me, all you who are weary and burdened, and I will give you rest" (Matthew 11:28). Or these life-engendering words: "Those who hope in the Lord will renew their strength. They will soar on wings like eagles; they will run and not grow weary, they will walk and not be faint" (Isaiah 40:31). Or this: "So do not throw away your confidence; it will be richly rewarded. You need to persevere so that when you have done the will of God, you will receive what he has promised. For in just a little while, 'He who is coming will come and will not delay. But my righteous one will live by faith' " (Hebrews 10:36-38). Jesus knew these truths by heart and this passion to listen to his Father caused him to give up his life willingly.

He Willingly Gave Up His Life

While attending school, we have to take tests to show how much we know. We have no choice. In the military, one must go through basic training to become a full-fledged soldier. No other way. To be an honorable citizen, we must file taxes each year — or risk getting in trouble. It's not an "if I feel like it" situation.

Jesus did something he didn't want to do and he did it willingly. No IRS agent was going to knock on his door if he didn't follow through on God's plan. Boot camp is a cakewalk compared to what Jesus submitted to. And Jesus walked into this test, yes, with trepidation, but with joy that was set before him. "I offered my back to those who beat me, my cheeks to those who pulled out my beard; I did not hide my face from mocking and spitting" (v. 6). Jesus wasn't forced to do this. He wasn't disobedient like Moses who objected, Jeremiah who made excuses, or Jonah who ran away. There was no rebellion or apostasy or hesitation on Jesus' part at all.

He set his face like flint — hard, unchanging, unbendable — towards Jerusalem. Nothing would stop him from finishing his task. Even if the disciples had risen up, it wouldn't deter him. Remember that he didn't even let an unattached ear cause a diversion and escape. Rather he reattached it. At the hardest moment of all, in the Garden of Gethsemane, his submitting words were, "Not my will, Father, but yours!" All because Jesus knew that it was

God's will that he suffer. The majesty of it all is that God, in Jesus, was in control the whole time. He let his life be taken away. Passionately he finished the calling because he didn't want himself or anyone else to be put to shame!

He Desires That No One Be Put To Shame

Have you ever had the medical opportunity to wear a Holter monitor? It's the computerized box that is attached to electrodes that are stuck to your chest to monitor your heart rhythms for a 24-hour period. It's completely painless except when they don't shave a hairy chest and stick the adhesive electrodes directly on the skin. A day later when the nurse removes those sticky analyzers, lots of hair stays with them. They pluck the hairs, a clump of hair, right out of the skin. That stings, but its not humiliating like the plucking of the beard Jesus went through out of hardened anger against him or the degradation of the spittle that ran down his face after one of the soldiers cleared his throat and let it fly. Utter contempt. Ignominy to the highest degree.

Yet, Jesus wasn't disgraced. The only shame for Jesus would have been resisting this and many other embarrassing indecencies that were done to him. He was not shamed, because he bore the weight of our sin all the way and was vindicated when he said, "It is finished," and gave up his life voluntarily. He was ultimately vindicated, by his dad, when he burst forth from the tomb three days later. Jesus understands shame. He went through it like no else ever will and his desire is that the one "who trusts in him will never be put to shame" (Romans 10:11).

There was a woman who had a problem. She had the worst case of bad breath ever smelled. Nothing she did — the sprays, the mints, the doctor's visits — seemed to help. This affected her personal relationships, especially with guys. She would never get close to them or let them kiss her.

There was a man who had another problem. He had the worst case of smelly feet ever smelled. He never removed his shoes and took great pains to wash his feet continually so even he could sleep with himself.

Yes, you guessed it. These two people met, and they started to date. Somehow through the months they hid their ailments from each other. She never opened her mouth to kiss, and he never took his shoes off, even when they went swimming. They were in love and decided to get married. On the wedding night, she was in the bathroom of the hotel crying hysterically, "What am I going to do?" He was in the room frantically trying to find a place to hide his shoes. Finally, she burst out of the bathroom sobbing and grabbed her new husband and blurted out, "I have a confession to make!" Without hesitation, he said, "Don't tell me: you ate my socks!"

That's a funny story, but shame is no laughing matter. Some of you have secrets like the newlyweds. Some of you have been falsely accused or betrayed by others. Shame engulfs others of you because of something perpetrated upon you. Others only hear the accuser Satan speaking to you right now: "You can never be forgiven! You'll never get rid of your shame!" Your Savior understands what it is like to be falsely accused, to have a finger pointing at you, to feel hurt, betrayal, and shame. Like Jesus, who hung naked on the cross, you feel naked and exposed, vulnerable and wary. You put on a good front and keep buying the newest mouthwash or Odoreaters. But nothing seems to take away the pain. Millions of hurting, shame-filled people in our world need freedom from guilt and fear.

The antidote to smelly feet and bad breath is Romans 8:1: "Therefore, there is now no condemnation for those who are in Christ Jesus." No accusation from the One who counts the most! Because Jesus in his passionate passion took your sin, bore your shame, and was even rejected by God, you are not rejected. God will never turn his back on you. His desire is that you are never ashamed!

What are you passionate about? Golf is a great way to get the competitive juices flowing and play in God's green world. Collecting pigs ... well, that's satisfying to some. And being passionate about life is a wonderful blessing. But I want to be passionate like Jesus. Especially this coming Holy Week. I want to hear my Father's voice. I want to lay down my life for others. And I want to tell the world, "Trust in Jesus and you will never be put to shame!"

Held In
His Arms

Isaiah 52:13—53:12

Years ago, there was a very wealthy man who, with his devoted young son, shared a passion for collecting art. Together they traveled around the world, adding only the finest art treasures to their collection. Priceless works by Picasso, Van Gogh, Monet, and many others adorned the walls of the family estate. The widowed elderly man looked on with satisfaction as his only child became an experienced art collector. The son's trained eye and sharp business mind caused his father to beam with pride as they dealt with art collectors around the world.

As winter approached, war engulfed the nation, and the young man left to serve his country. After only a few short weeks, his father received a telegram. His beloved son was missing in action. The art collector awaited more news, fearing he would never see his son again. Within days, his fears were confirmed. The young man had died while rushing a fellow soldier to a medic.

Distraught and lonely, the old man faced the upcoming holidays with anguish and sadness. The joy of the season, that he and his son had always looked forward to, would visit his house no longer.

One morning, a knock on the door awakened the depressed old man. When he opened the door, a soldier greeted him with a large package in his hands. He introduced himself to the man by saying, "I was a friend of your son. I was the one he was rescuing when he died. May I come in for a few moments? I have something to show you."

As the two began to talk, the soldier told of how the man's son had told everyone of his, not to mention his father's, love of fine art. "I am an artist," said the soldier, "and I want to give you this."

As the old man unwrapped the package, the paper gave way to reveal a portrait of the man's son. Though the world would never consider it the work of a genius, the painting featured the young man's face in stirring detail. Overcome with emotion, the man thanked the soldier, promising to hang the picture above the fireplace. A few hours later, after the soldier had departed, the old man set about his task. True to his word, the painting went above the fireplace, pushing aside thousands of dollars worth of art. The old man sat in his chair and spent the rest of the holiday gazing at the gift he had been given.

On this holy, somber Good Friday we talk about another Son who gave his life for us. (We'll finish our story later.) To understand the sacrifice he delivered to us, I ask you to do something you've never done in church before: make a muscle. That's right, I want all of you to raise your arms up and pretend you are bragging to someone about how big your muscles are. Thank you. You may put your arms down.

Children do that all the time. In front of others. In front of the mirror. "Look how big my arm is, Mom and Dad." With the stress on becoming and staying fit in today's world, big biceps are "in." "Hey, honey, look how big and strong and firm my arms are!"

How big are God's arms? What do God's arms look like?

I don't know what they look like, but I do know what they do. "Sing to the Lord a new song, for he has done marvelous things; his right hand and his holy arm have worked salvation for him" (Psalm 98:1). "You saw with your own eyes the great trials, the miraculous signs and wonders, the mighty hand and outstretched arm, with which the Lord your God brought you out" (Deuteronomy 8:17). God's arms must boast very powerful biceps!

The arm of the Lord is his power and might and vengeance. He does whatever he pleases, whenever he pleases. I want to show you how God flexed his muscles on our behalf and displayed his powerful arms in our text on this Holy Weekend.

First, *the arm of the Lord formed the Son* (v. 2). Jesus grew up before his Father "like a tender shoot" after God's Spirit overshadowed Mary and she began to carry Jesus in her womb. Just as God is actively involved in the formation of each embryo in the womb (and even before that in his mind), so imagine the joy God received seeing the arms and legs of his Son grow inside Mary. It is God who first gave Jesus physical arms with which to hold the children the disciples had shooed away and the arms that made the mud which he put on the blind man's eyes.

Second, *the arm of the Lord struck the Son* (v. 4). Though through the 33 years of his life, God was delighted to watch Jesus grow in wisdom and stature, now the power of God afflicted his Son. The powerful arm of God came down in the fists of the soldiers who struck him and in the pounding of the reed they used to force the crown of thorns into his head. It was God's outstretched arms that inflicted the 39 lashes as Jesus was tied to a pillar. God's might was used to hurt his Son so we consider "him stricken by God, smitten by him." Jesus put his arms down and refused to fight.

Third, *the arm of the Lord pierced the Son* (v. 5). They will look on the one they have pierced. Not exactly correct. There's no "they" about it. "He" pierced his Son with the spikes that were driven into his hands and feet and the angry spear that was thrust into his side. If you doubt it was the arm of the Lord, hear verse 10: "Yet it was the Lord's will to crush him and cause him to suffer!" God desired it. For our transgressions!

Fourth, *the arm of the Lord cut off the Son* (v. 8). When Jesus agonized and died on the cross, he went through literal hell. Not just the "hell" we say we endure in a tragedy, but actual Satan-controlled and damning hell. God "cut him off" because he cannot be tainted with the evil of hell and sin. Jesus was also "cut off" from those who are living. His outstretched arms went limp and he breathed no more.

Fifth, *the arm of the Lord raised him up* (v. 11). This is Easter on Good Friday. After suffering our death, God promised that Jesus would see the light of life again. The soldiers put a seal on the tomb and the devil had chalked up another victim, but God's power moved the stone, enlivened the dead and "exalted him to the highest place and gave him the name that is above every name." The upraised hands of Jesus signaled victory as he ascended back to his Father.

Does God still use his arms to demonstrate his power today? Yes. Usually to lift us up and place us on solid footing again. What if you fell into a pit and there was no way out by yourself. A **subjective person** would come along and say, "I feel for you down there." An **objective person** would look at you and say, "It's logical that you would fall down there." A **mathematician** would calculate how you fell into the pit. A **news reporter** would want the exclusive story on the pit. An **IRS agent** would ask you if you were paying taxes on your pit. **Confucius** would look at you and say, "A wise person would not walk so near the pit to fall in." A **self-pitying person** would moan, "You haven't seen anything until you've seen my pit!" A **fire-and-brimstone preacher** would bellow, "You deserve your pit!"

Buddha would come by and say, "Your desires make you want out. Change your desires." A **Hindu** would tell you, "You just think you are miserable in the pit; change your thinking." A **psychologist** would counsel: "You mother and father are to blame for your being in that pit." A **self-esteem therapist** would say, "If you had self-esteem, you could get out of your pit." An **optimist** would smile and say, "Things could be worse." A **pessimist** would groan, "Things will get worse!"

Jesus, seeing you in the pit, reaches down, takes you by the hand and lifts you out of the pit.

He grabs you with his outstretched arm, lifts you up, and walks beside you so you never fall in the pit again. With those same arms he hugs you and says, "You are my child. I love you. With you I am well-pleased!" And when you stumble or begin to fall, Jesus whispers into your ears, "Fear not!" Because of the power shown in the arm of the Lord against Jesus, underneath you are "the everlasting arms"!

We conclude our story about the art collector father. During the days and weeks that followed his son's death, the man realized that even though his son was no longer with him, the boy's life would live on because of those he had touched. He soon learned that his son had rescued dozens of wounded soldiers before a bullet took his life.

As the stories of his son's gallantry continued to reach him, fatherly pride and satisfaction began to ease his grief. The painting of his son soon became his most prized possession, far eclipsing any interest in the pieces for which museums around the world clamored. He told his neighbors it was the greatest gift he had ever received.

The following spring, the old man became ill and died. The art world was in anticipation that with the collector's passing and his only son dead those paintings would be sold at auction.

The day soon arrived and art collectors from around the world gathered to bid on some of the world's most spectacular paintings. Dreams would be fulfilled this day; greatness would be achieved as many would hope to claim, "I have the greatest collection."

The auction began with a painting that was not on any museum's list. It was the painting of the man's son. The auctioneer asked for an opening bid, but the room was silent. "Who will open the bidding with $100?" he asked. Minutes passed, and no one spoke. From the back of the room came a voice, "Who cares about that painting? It's just a picture of his son." "Let's forget about it and move on to the good stuff," more voices echoed in agreement.

"No, we have to sell this one first," replied the auctioneer. "Now, who will take the son?" Finally a neighbor of the old man spoke. "Will you take ten dollars for the painting? That's all I have. I knew the boy so I'd like to have it."

"I have ten dollars. Will anyone go higher?" called the auctioneer. After more silence, the auctioneer said, "Going once, going twice, gone." The gavel fell. Cheers filled the room and someone exclaimed, "Now we can get on with it and bid on the real treasures!"

The auctioneer looked at the audience and announced that the auction was over. Stunned disbelief quieted the room. Someone spoke up and asked, "What do mean, it's over? We didn't come here for a picture of some old guy's son. What about all these paintings? There are millions of dollars worth of art here! I demand that you explain what is going on!"

The auctioneer replied, "It's very simple. According to the will of the father, whoever takes the son ... gets it all!"

Till Death Do Us — Unite

Isaiah 25:6-9 or Acts 10:34-43

Pastor: Christ is risen!
People: He is risen, indeed!

Pastor: Death is a disgrace!
People: Not any more!

Pastor: Jesus lives and conquered death!
People: I will never die.

Pastor: No more tears!
People: No more fears!

All: Praise be to the Death Conqueror!

God had done miraculous things for her and her family through the Prophet Elijah. Enough flour and oil to live on through a drought. Then this widow's son became sick. He eventually died. "Why, O prophet, have you let this happen?" she asked. But God wasn't done bestowing miracles on this family. Elijah, harboring the same question for God, stretched himself on the boy three times — and he became a fence-climbing, dog-chasing son again!

A second widow had heard about all the miracles the Prophet Jesus was doing. But it didn't do her any good. Her only son died. She was alone. That is, until Jesus crashed their funeral procession and told the boy to get up off the funeral bier — and he ran to give his mother a hug!

53

Two sisters couldn't believe that this miracle-working friend, who claimed to be God, had delayed coming to them when their brother was sick. But now it was too late. He'd been in the rock-hewn tomb three days. Who could help them now? Smelly, decomposing, hidden-in-the-earth problems didn't phase Jesus — and Lazarus lived again!

Can you imagine talking to the two nameless widows' sons and Lazarus, who received new leases on life? What did they see? How did it feel really to die and then to have your brain start waving again? Were they glad they were back? Did they see God? What exactly happens when you die, Lazarus and sons?

We don't know the answers to those questions, but we do understand this: all three of these guys have one thing in common. They died again — and any questions they still had in their second life about death were answered. There is only one person who died and came back to life again, never to die again!

He will remain the only person, that is, until our Easter text is fulfilled in all Christians' lives someday.

When the Old Testament people heard this Scripture read in their worship services, all they could think of was some abstract eternity with God somewhere. All their hope was future-oriented. A mountain banquet. No more death. No more fear. Salvation. When they heard about a mountain with a banquet for all peoples, they envisioned a heavenly Mount Zion, a holy happy place where the buffet lines never end. When they heard about no more death and no more tears, they could only imagine their eternity as that wonderful. And when they were called to "rejoice and be glad in his salvation" (v. 9), they only pondered his ultimate salvation: their gift of heaven — someday! All future. No immediate fulfillment. Only something to look forward to.

As New Testament Christians, especially on Easter, we have more than just something to look forward to, but something to celebrate now! Today! This passage has been fulfilled already. It has present power and future promises! The mountain God spoke of was not just Mount Zion, but Friday's Mount Calvary. As a result of what happened there, we can rejoice and party and banquet today on Christ's body and blood as a foretaste of the feast to come!

The blood shed on that mountain doesn't just guarantee us eternal life, but a life free from the fear of death now! The wiping away of all tears is not just at heaven's gate ("check all your tears over there — next to the coat check!"), but now. If Jesus can conquer death, he can handle our problems too! And our salvation is present tense, today, already fulfilled because the Savior walks by our side!

This exhilarating text has been and will be fulfilled in our life and death and life again!

In the popular comic strip *Crankshaft*, one box-strip has Crankshaft carrying a shovel and walking with his grandson after burying their pet dog. The grandson asks, "Where do we go when we die, Gramps?" All Crankshaft answers is, "Away." "How far away?" "Depends ..." "On what?" "Lots of things." The grandson replies, "Thanks, Gramps ..." "No problem." Too bad the comic sketcher didn't talk about the cross he drew sticking out of the mound of dirt! I guess it wouldn't make a good comic strip to show the cross as the bar across the door of hell. "Sorry, Jesus closed hell." Now the grave is the open door to heaven!

Death Is A Disgrace — If That's All There Is!

Death is a disgrace because it is the ultimate vulnerability. In front of people. Before God. What can a dead person do? Nothing. Think about a person lying in a casket with everyone parading by. Finally the CEO is not in charge anymore; he can't make decisions any more. Others will make decisions for him. Everyone sees him as he really is, no matter what the undertaker's makeup tries to cover. At death there's no more bamboozling about the real faults of the person, no more lying to oneself about his rough edges. If there is ever a moment of weakness, it's at death — if that's all there is!

That's why Isaiah calls death "the shroud that enfolds all people, the sheet that covers all nations" (v. 7). No one escapes, all nations will die, and we are covered up. The shroud refers to what the executioner puts over the condemned man's face before the rope is pulled or the switch flipped. We are all condemned people, "for the wages of sin is death." Death was a disgrace for Jesus, too, hanging naked on the cross. That's why they had to get him off before the Sabbath sundown.

But death isn't all there is. Death for the Christian, though unpleasant to go through, is really just that, a "going through" to the other side. A bank in Binghamton, New York, had some flowers sent to a competitor who had recently moved into a new building. There was a mix-up at the flower shop, and the card sent with the arrangement read, "With our deepest sympathy."

The florist, who was greatly embarrassed, apologized. But he was even more embarrassed when he realized that the card intended for the bank was attached to a floral arrangement sent to a funeral home in honor of a deceased person. That card read, "Congratulation on your new location!" Ah, how appropriate for Christians who die.

Jesus Collects Your Tears

There was once a contest held to find out who the most caring child was. The winner was a four-year-old child whose next door neighbor was an elderly man who had recently lost his wife. Upon seeing the man cry, the little boy went into the old gentleman's yard, climbed onto his lap, and just sat there. When his mother asked him what he had said to the neighbor, the little boy said, "Nothing, I just helped him cry."

We cry when a loved one dies. And rightly so. Can you name all of the people who were crying and grieving when Jesus died? The women ran to the tomb crying. Peter wept bitterly for his denial and the fact that Jesus would die. The two men on the road to Emmaus, if not shedding physical tears, surely had their hearts broken. And perhaps you today are crying — if not outside, then inside. Jesus cares about your tears and promises one day to wipe them all away (v. 8). But for now, hear Psalm 56:8: "Record my lament; list my tears on your scroll — are they not in your record?" God collects our tears in a bottle. He counts and knows all your sorrows. Jesus' resurrection is the Divine Handkerchief today, because we know that those who die in Christ we will see again, and until then God wipes our tears!

Death Will Be No More

Nothing is ever final on this earth. Satan thought he had vanquished the Son of God when he breathed his last, but nothing was over — except Satan's reign of terror with death as his ultimate weapon. When Jesus died he killed death. Yes, death still bites (we die physically), but Jesus took away its sting and the venom of its hopelessness and the bitterness of hell. Because our Redeemer lives, we will stand on the earth. Jesus has freed those who all their lives were held in slavery by their fear of death. Death is only the message that calls us home, not a prison warden that drags us to doom. No, heaven is a party!

The sound of Sarah's voice on the other end of the telephone always brought a smile to Pastor Neal's face. This time, however, there seemed to be an unusual tone to her words, "Pastor, could you stop by this afternoon? I need to talk with you." "Of course, I'll be there around three. Is that okay?"

It didn't take long for Pastor Neal to discover the reason for what he had only sensed in her voice earlier. Sarah shared the news that her doctor had discovered a previously undetected tumor. "He says I probably have about six months to live." Sarah's words were naturally serious, yet there was a definite calm about her. "I'm so sorry ..." but before the pastor could finish, Sarah interrupted. "Don't be. Jesus has been good. I have lived a long life. I'm ready to go."

"I know," Pastor Neal whispered with a reassuring nod.

"But I do want to talk with you about my funeral. I have been thinking about it and there are things that I know I want." The two talked quietly for a long time. When it seemed that they had covered just about everything, Sarah paused, looked up at her pastor with a twinkle in her eye, and then added, "One more thing. When they bury me, I want my old Bible in one hand and a fork in the other."

"A fork?" Neal was sure he had heard everything, but this caught him by surprise. "Why do you want to be buried with a fork?"

"I have been thinking about all the church dinners that I attended through the years," she explained. "Sometimes, at the best ones, somebody would lean over my shoulder and whisper, 'You can keep your fork.' And do you know what that meant? Dessert was coming! And not a cup of Jell-O or pudding or even a dish of ice cream. You don't need a fork for that. It meant the good stuff, like chocolate cake or cherry pie. When they told me to keep my fork, I knew the best was yet to come!

"That's exactly what I want people to talk about at my funeral. Sure they can talk about all the good times we had. That would be nice. But when they walk by my casket and look at my pretty blue dress, I want them to turn to one another and say, 'Why the fork?'

"That's when I want you to tell them that I kept my fork because the best is yet to come!"

The best *is* yet to come. We'll get to talk with Lazarus and the two boys. We'll see our family members who have died knowing Jesus. Best of all, we'll meet our Savior face to face and he will serve us at the never-ending feast. A blessed Easter to you! Come, Lord Jesus, come!

Open Grave, Open Hearts

Acts 4:32-35

As the Cadillac owner walked to his car, he saw a boy about ten years old staring intently through the windows. Wondering what he was up to, the man put his hands on the youngster's shoulders, pulled gently and asked him what he was doing. The boy said he was interested in cars and had read a lot about different models. The owner talked with the boy for a while explaining to him details about this particular model and style.

After a little while, the boy asked, "Mister, how much did you pay for this car?" The man replied, "Nothing. My brother gave it to me." The boy responded, "I wish ..." but stopped without finishing. The man chuckled, "You were going to say, 'I wish I had a brother like that.'"

"No, I was going to say, 'I wish I could *be* a brother like that.' You see, sir, I have a brother who is crippled and I'd like to do a lot of things for him."

Our text says, "All the believers were one in heart and mind. No one claimed that any of his possessions was his own, but they shared everything they had."

Jesus is alive! Christ is risen! The grave is open; so also are our hearts and hands!

A sermon on giving at Easter time? I thought that was an emphasis for fall. Why *not* now? Giving should be our response to Jesus' life, death, and life again. Not just replanting lilies in the garden, dry-cleaning your suit to store for next year, or finding places to store egg baskets and that elusive green and pink grass. The grave is open; so also are our hearts and hands!

Note that in the middle of our assigned text, there is emphasis on preaching by the disciples about the living Jesus and "much grace was upon them!" Sounds like our worship services on Saturdays and Sundays. Jesus is present in his Word and Sacraments, so there is grace present. But isn't it interesting that these words on the Word and divine favor are sandwiched between verses on giving, sharing, selling goods — all to help those in need?

How did the people of Jerusalem and Palestine know that Jesus really was alive? There were more than 5,000 followers of the Way by then. But it wasn't only by the testifying of the apostles. It wasn't only by the joy on the faces of Thomas and Bartholomew. It wasn't only the empty tomb and not only the power the Risen Lord gave to the disciples at Pentecost. Above all else, the living Jesus was demonstrated by their giving spirit, their care for the less fortunate!

A man complained to his pastor, "I've been listening to your sermons and to our leaders at church and what you are asking us to do here and in our community is getting to be just one continuous 'give, give, give.'" To which the pastor replied, "Say, that's one of the best descriptions of Christianity I've ever heard!"

The early Church understood this. Our society has lost much of what the early Church had, including the desire to find a need and fill it, especially in the social ministry area. This text does not promote communism or bringing everyone down to the lowest level or even equal levels. It does promote taking care of others in the name of Jesus. The early Church was a small family. They were misunderstood and considered a sect. Even with the grace of God upon them, they had to stick together. So, "from time to time" they sold lands and property. Though not forced to, they did so once in a while. They didn't give all their money to a common pot. Their unity was expressed in reaching out, in thinking of others. It wasn't dinners or proclamations or cliques that they were known for (though that would have been easy) but for helping the community of believers.

What if they had not done this as the apostles testified? What if they had not responded to the grace upon them? Would people have believed? The grave was opened. Now their hearts and hands were open!

What about us? Do people see God for who he really is by what they see in you and me? Or are we more like cute, adorable, and selfish children who want their things when they want them? The following is a Toddler's Creed, by an unknown author:

> *If I want it, it's mine.*
> *If I give it to you, and change my mind later, it's mine.*
> *If I can take it way from you, it's mine.*
> *If I had it a little while ago, it's mine.*
> *If it's mine, it will never belong to anyone else, no matter what.*
> *If we are building something together, all the pieces are mine.*
> *If it looks just like mine, it is mine!*

Or do we do grown-up things like the notorious miser who was called on by the chairman of the community charity? "Sir," said the fund-raiser, "our records show that despite your wealth, you've never once given to our drive."

"Do your records show that I have an elderly mother who was left penniless when my father died?" fumed the tightwad. "Do your records show that I have a disabled brother who is unable to work? Do your records show that I have a widowed sister with small children who can barely make ends meet?"

"No, sir," replied the embarrassed volunteer. "Our records don't show those things."

"Well, I don't give to any of them, so why should I give anything to you?"

Or do we know the truth of Saint Paul's encouragement to the church in Corinth in this second letter about a giving heart? "But just as you excel in everything — in faith, in speech, in knowledge, in complete earnestness, and in your love for us — see that you also excel in this grace of giving ... for you know the grace of our Lord Jesus Christ, that though he was rich, yet for your sakes he became poor, so that you through his poverty might become rich" (8:7, 9).

When Jesus gets ahold of our life and we know the power of his resurrection, we act like he did: giving and serving, not being served. In fact, the Holy Spirit in response to an open heart can enable us to give not only money to the church, bread and canned goods to the local pantry, and our muscle to build Habitat for Humanity homes, but also our very lives so that others may know the Crucified and Risen Christ. Some people will never come to know Jesus until they see us getting down and dirty for them, giving up some of our comforts (as the Lord calls us). Then they will finally see Jesus-with-skin-on. Not even our homes and property are to be more important than the opportunities to show the resurrected Jesus to a dying world. "However, I consider my life worth nothing to me, if only I may finish the race and complete the task the Lord Jesus has given me — the task of testifying to the gospel of God's grace" (Acts 20:24).

How can I share my Easter faith this week with someone in need? Where is grace upon us as a congregation that would enable us to reach out more than we are already doing? How can we fulfill the two great commands of our Resurrected Lord to love God with all that is within us and to love our neighbor as ourselves?

It's just one big "give, give, give," pastor! Yes, it is, when you know Jesus and all he's given us: forgiveness, release from fear of death, abundant life, power over the devil, peace, and joy! He lives! We give! We live and give for him!

Ruth Peterson reached out her door to get her mail. A very plain looking envelope caught her attention first. It had no return address. Inside it was a one page letter with these few words written on it: "Dear Ruth, I'm going to be in your neighborhood Saturday afternoon and I'd like to stop by for a visit." And it was signed, "Love always, Jesus."

Her hands were shaking as she placed the letter on her kitchen table. "Why would the Lord want to visit me? I'm nobody special. I don't have anything to offer." With that thought, Ruth remembered her empty kitchen cabinets. "Oh my goodness, I really don't have anything to offer. I'll have to run down to the store and buy something for dinner." She reached for her purse and counted out its contents: $5.40. "Well, I can get some bread and cold cuts, at least."

She threw on her coat and hurried out the door. A loaf of French bread, a half-pound of sliced turkey, and a carton of milk. That left Ruth with a grand total of twelve cents to last her until Monday. Nonetheless she felt happy as she headed home, her meager offering tucked under her arm.

"Hey, lady, can you help us, lady?" Ruth had been so absorbed in her dinner plan, she hadn't even noticed two figures huddled in the alleyway, a man and a woman, both of them dressed in little more than rags. "Look, lady, I ain't got a job, ya know, and my wife and I have been living out here on the street, and, well, now it's getting cold and we're getting kinda hungry and, well, if you could help us, lady, we'd really appreciate it."

Ruth looked at them both. They were dirty, they smelled bad and, frankly, she was certain that they could get some kind of work if they really wanted to. "Sir, I'd like to help you, but I'm a poor woman myself. All I have is a few cold cuts and some bread, and I'm having an important guest for dinner tonight and I was planning on serving that to him."

"Yeah, well, okay, lady, I understand. Thanks anyway." The man put his arm around the woman's shoulders, turned and headed back into the alley. As she watched them leave, Ruth felt a familiar twinge in her heart.

"Sir, wait!" The couple stopped and turned as she ran down the alley after them. "Look, why don't you take this food? I'll figure out something else to serve my guest." She handed the man her grocery bag. "Thank you, lady. Thank you very much!" "Yes, thank you!" It was the man's wife, and Ruth could see now that she was shivering. "You know, I've got another coat at home. Here, why don't you take this one?" Ruth unbuttoned her jacket and slipped it over the woman's shoulders. Then smiling, she turned and walked back down the street ... without her coat and nothing to serve her guest.

Ruth was chilled by the time she reached her front door, and worried too. The Lord was coming to visit and she didn't have anything to offer him. She fumbled through her purse for the door key. But as she did, she noticed another envelope in her mailbox.

"That's odd. The mailman doesn't usually come twice in one day." She took the envelope out of the box and opened it.

"Dear Ruth, it was good to see you again. Thank you for the lovely meal. And thank you, too, for the beautiful coat. Love always, Jesus."

The air was still cold, but even without her coat, Ruth no longer noticed.

Jesus is alive! Christ is risen! The grave is open; so also are our hearts and hands!

What Are You Looking At?

Acts 3:12-19

We are living in the days of the apostles again. We are the early Church all over again — or, more precisely, we live in a similar spiritual environment in which the Church first grew. What do I mean? I don't say this because of miracles and prophecies being fulfilled in the same way they were back then. Nor because sin is so prevalent and accepted, even as it was in the Roman Empire. Nor do I say it because we, like the 5,000 plus who grew to millions and millions, are waiting eagerly and expecting Jesus to come back soon.

No, we are living in the days of the apostles again because just as the message of a crucified, risen Messiah was so new and misunderstood then, so it is now. Just as only a minority knew and believed that the Christ had come, so now few people have really heard about Jesus or truly believe in him. And as in the days of Peter and Paul, people are awaiting a Messiah: a financial Christ, a political messiah, and a savior from whatever ails them. In this post-Christian era in which we live and work, the text for today is dynamic and alive. It's a simple message, but is that not what the apostles preached back then?

What we need is the boldness of Peter to say three things as he seizes their moment of wonder: 1) Don't look at us (v. 12); 2) Look at God and his Son (vv. 13-18); 3) Look at yourself (vv. 17,19).

Why did Peter stand up and say all this? He said it because a spectacular miracle had just occurred right outside the temple. A man no longer begged there for money; now he was jumping and shouting for joy. No longer did the people of the city look on him with pity, but with wide-eyed amazement. He was no longer crippled, but his feet and ankles were strong. He was healed and he was clinging to Peter and John. Peter says:

Don't Look At Us

After seeing this undeniable miracle and its result, the people, even as today always looking for miracles and heroes, came running to them looking for what else these two men with such great power could do. "Don't look at us," said Peter, "we didn't do anything!"

Later on in Acts, Simon the sorcerer did the same thing after he became a Christian. He thought he could buy the ability to impart the Holy Spirit to people. Peter had to tell him, "Don't look at us — it is a gift from God!" And Paul encountered the same human adoration when he and Barnabas also healed a crippled man. The priest of the pagan temple honoring Zeus was all set to offer sacrifices until Paul told them, "Don't look at us!"

Even when God uses us to do great exploits in his kingdom this should be our attitude. It's not me. It's Jesus! Jumbo the elephant and Flick the flea were long-time great friends. They often walked and chatted together. Actually, they were inseparable. One day they were walking along a back-country road when they came to a flimsy wooden bridge that spanned a deep gorge. They walked across, the little bridge swaying and creaking under the weight of the elephant. When they were across, the flea asked his big friend, "Did you notice how we shook that bridge?"

Even as powerful as Paul was, he was confident of this: "Not that we are competent in ourselves to claim anything for ourselves, but our competence comes from God" (2 Corinthians 3:5). I love juxtaposing these two verses as I quote them to myself each morning in the shower: "Apart from God I can do nothing!" yet "I can do all things through Christ who strengthens me!"

"Men of Israel, why does this surprise you? We work for Jesus!"

Look At The Son

Look at the names humble Peter and John used to describe their Master in our text: God's servant, Holy and Righteous One,

Author of Life, and God's Christ. Far short of promoting themselves, they lifted up Jesus' name and gave us names which describe his purpose and beauty.

Peter and John didn't try to impress their listeners, they just spoke the truth about Jesus. "He's not dead anymore. His Father said, 'Get up, arise!' And he did. It is his resurrected power that enabled us to be conduits for the miracle you just viewed. Why do you stare at us as if by our own power or godliness we had made this man walk?"

Our entire ministry, all our talking, all our planning — and any bragging we do — must lift up Jesus. More than that, our whole lives should be lived as if we are Jesus-with-skin-on!

A little boy about ten years old was standing before a shoe store on Broadway in New York City, barefooted, peering through the window, and shivering with cold. It was December. A lady approached the boy and said, "My little fellow, why are you looking so earnestly in that window?"

"I was asking God to give me a pair of shoes," was the boy's reply.

The lady took him by the hand and went into the store and asked the clerk to get half a dozen pairs of socks for the boy. Then she asked if he could give her a basin of water and a towel. He quickly brought them to her. She took the little fellow to the back part of the store and, removing her gloves, knelt down, washed his little feet, and dried them with a towel.

By this time the clerk had returned with the socks. Placing a pair upon the boy's feet, she purchased him a pair of shoes, and tying up the remaining socks, gave them to him. She patted him on the head and said, "No doubt, my little fellow, you feel more comfortable now?"

As she turned to go, the astonished lad caught her by the hand, and looking up in her face, with tears in his eyes, answered the question with these words, "Are you God's wife?"

Look At Yourself

When we've taken the focus off of us and put it on the One who died for all, then we can rightly tell all listeners to look inside themselves and see what God is saying to them. Peter didn't just tell his listeners to consider doing so; he made them do it. And he wasn't really gentle about it. He displayed early church boldness to confront the people with their sin.

He minced no words when he said: You disowned Jesus. You killed Life. Then Peter gave three exhibits whom the people despised or looked down upon. He said, "They are more righteous than you." **Exhibit one** is Pilate. Yes, he gets the public blame and his name is even in the historic Apostle's Creed, but he's better than you are. You disowned God's Son before Pilate, "though he had decided to let him go!" You used him as a scapegoat, men of Israel, but not anymore. All the guilt is yours. Look at you — you're more guilty than despicable Pilate!

But wait, there's more: **Exhibit two** is murderous Barabbas who was freed from condemnation instead of Jesus. And you, men of Israel, asked for him. "You disowned the Holy and Righteous one and asked that a murderer be released to you. How could you?" Peter grieves. You set a filthy insurrectionist free and casually murdered the Christ. Look at yourself — you're worse than Barabbas!

Peter wasn't done with his scathing rebuke. He held up one more exhibit to show the people how far they had strayed. **Exhibit three:** Peter points to the man just healed. It is by faith in the name of Jesus that he is well; faith in Jesus is why this man is walking around. He has something you don't have and you need it. You're crippled in your spirit. Only Jesus can heal you too, but you must trust in him. Look at yourself — will you believe like this high stepping, dancing man?

The story is told of a little girl whose mother planned to celebrate her fifth birthday by impressing all the relatives. The mother dressed her daughter in her Sunday best and said, "Now here is what I want you to do. You're going to sing a song."

When it was time for the little girl to sing, her mother said, "Honey, what are you going to do?" The child said, "Nothing." The mother found a convenient spot to pinch her and said, "Weren't you going to sing?" The child said, "No."

The angry mother took the child upstairs and shut her in a closet. About a half an hour later the mother went up and said, "What are you doing up here?"

The child said, "I've been having a great time. I've been spitting on your clothes. I've been spitting on your shoes. I've been spitting on your walls. I've been spitting on the carpet. Now I'm waiting for some more spit."

Look inside yourself and you will find ignorance and lack of knowledge. Peter is bold in addressing sin, yet like the Savior, he also is bold in extending mercy. You might be ignorant and guilty, but there is hope. You might be rebellious and scornful, but there's hope. You might even love to spit. Look at the cross you built and filled. Look at what your sin did and there find forgiveness if you will but turn to God. The very things you are guilty of are why Jesus died.

Our text says that your sins will be wiped out! What good news! No more washing our hands like Pilate. No more Barabbas guilt. And the healed man's faith is lacking no longer. Do you know what it means for sins to be wiped out? It doesn't mean it was crumpled up and thrown away. Wiped out does not mean saved in a file only God can find on his computer. Sin is not even burned in a fire where only ashes remain.

When Jesus died on the cross and when we are forgiven at Baptism or on our faith birthday, it's as if our sins, which were written in black on an erasable memo board, are forever erased with no shadows or residue remaining. It's a brand new board! What Peter's hearers thought of was the precursor to the modern kitchen's memo board. In those day's scribes wrote on papyrus and the ink used had no acid in it. Therefore it did not sink into the papyrus, like our modern ink does. One could simply take a sponge and wipe it away. Colossians 2:13-14 says, "He forgave us all our sins, having cancelled the written code, with its regulations, that was against us and that stood opposed to us; he took it away, nailing it to the cross."

Who do you know that is ignorant to the claims and truth of Jesus? There are plenty in this day of the apostles renewed. Ignorance is not an excuse, but it does give us a beautiful opportunity to tell others the truth. As the airplane was filling with passengers before takeoff, a lady saw a vacant seat beside a preacher. "Is this seat saved?" she asked. "I don't know," he replied, "but I am. Sit down and let me tell you about it."

It's not me. It's Jesus! And you need him!

No Apology

Acts 4:5-12

Sometimes it just takes boldness!

"Tell me what my dreams means," bellowed the king. "And I want to know what the dream was, too! It was so terrifying that I can't remember it! Tell me now! If you don't, O wise men of Babylon, I will have all of you killed."

That's the report Daniel heard in his prison cell as henchmen came to fulfill the king's earnest decree. "Wait, there's a God in heaven who reveals mysteries," delays Daniel, and with boldness in God and with confidence that God gives dream meanings, Daniel tells Nebuchadnezzar about the future.

Much later Daniel is put in a similar situation with the same king, but this time the dream is personally devastating to king Neb. When Daniel heard the dream this time, it terrified him. "My lord, if only the dream applied to your enemies and its meaning to your adversaries!" Daniel went on to describe a time of judgment upon the king that would turn him into a wild animal foraging in the wilderness. But Daniel told it anyway. Daniel always told the truth — no matter the bold cost.

So did Saint Peter. Last week we saw Peter trying to convince the Jewish people assembled around a healed man that their only hope was Jesus. Today he has a tougher audience, a much more critical and learned one. In fact 71 of the most wealthy, most intellectual, and most powerful rulers in the land were all ears to hear what Peter had to say. We might have retired pastors and academicians in our congregation, along with influential, well-off people, but we certainly do not have all the Congressmen, the majority of the American Bar Association and the elected leaders of the National Council of Churches. Yet this didn't stop Peter.

The rulers (administrators of the temple), the elders (heads of principal aristocratic families), and the teachers of the law (lawyers) all glared at Peter and said, "What gives you the right — what name, what power — to heal a crippled man? Who is behind you?"

Peter simply (no, not really, because he was empowered by the Holy Spirit) does two things: he points to the crippled man who is no longer so, and he points to Jesus who made him well. Peter declares salvation is only from him!

Ponder his courage. This is the first time that Christians were brought before a jury. This is the commencement of all the trials and hearings of Christians throughout the ages who have been tried because of Jesus' name. And this story is more meaningful because Peter is fulfilling Scripture even before it's written. He's writing Scripture even before he helped Mark write the second Gospel! He is given boldness to say what the Spirit gives him, even as he is questioned. Mark 13:11 says, "When you are arrested and brought to trial, do not worry beforehand about what to say. Just say whatever is given you at the time, for it is not you speaking, but the Holy Spirit."

And because it was God speaking, look who is in charge of this trial. Peter was teaching the teachers, not the other way around. The one on trial is admonishing the lawyers, not the lawyers condemning the criminal. And if you wonder if this took nerve, remember this is the same court that condemned Peter's Savior to death.

Then Peter does something we all can learn from. He moves the discussion from the sensation of healing to the hope of salvation. He quotes the Scripture these learned men know well from Psalms to get to the main point of his closing arguments: "Jesus was predicted a long time ago. Witness this psalm. He's the stone. You crucified him, but God raised him from the dead. He healed this man's legs and only he can heal you spiritually."

Someone has written about Jesus: "He who is the Bread of Life began his ministry hungering. He who is the Water of Life ended his ministry thirsting. Christ hungered as man, yet fed the hungry as God. He was weary, yet he is our rest. He paid tribute, yet he is the King. He was called a devil, but he cast out demons. He prayed, yet he hears our prayer. He wept. And he dries our tears. He was sold for thirty pieces of silver, yet he redeems sinners. He was led as a lamb to the slaughter, yet he is the Good Shepherd. He gave his life, and by dying he destroyed death." "*Salvation* is found in no one else, for there is *no other name* under heaven given to men by which we *must be saved!*"

Salvation: I wonder how many people in the world feel like Annas and company when this religious prisoner started preaching at them. Maybe like a scared Nebuchadnezzar. Or a convicted Agrippa preached to by another prisoner named Paul. Or just like the cubicle partner you work next to or the neighbor down the street when they hear that Jesus is the only way to heaven. "Oh, c'mon, don't be so closed-minded. You're showing your rigidity. You don't actually believe that, do you? You're being other-godphobic. How can you be so sure your god is the only way?"

Annas didn't believe that he needed to be saved. After all, they were Jews, God's chosen people, all right spiritually just because they were descendents of Abraham. Who is this brazen fool telling us we need to be saved? Salvation is from a condemned criminal who died recently?

Peter was breaking new ground, proclaiming good news that had never been heard before. A Messiah for everyone. You need him. He wants you. And you can't do it yourself. It is kind of like today when those who live in a supposed Christian nation believe that all good people will go to heaven, or perhaps all people will go to heaven, because how could God send anyone to hell?

How often have you heard these arguments against the need for outside salvation?

• If I am sincere, God will accept me.
• All the main religions lead to the same God anyway.
• If I believe in God and do some good things, I will make it.
• I'm not as bad as my neighbor. That must count for something!

No, you must be saved. Saved from yourself. Saved from the devil! And rescued from the world! How?

No other name: Between moments of dispensing wisdom, it seems that historical religious leaders had also learned software programming. One day, a great contest was held to test their skills. After days and days of fierce competition, only two leaders remained for the last day's event: Jesus and Mohammed.

The judge described the software application required for the final test, and gave the signal to start writing code. The two contestants feverishly typed away on their keyboards. Routines, applets, and applications flew by on their screens at incredible speeds. Windows, dialogs, and other intricate graphics began forming on their monitors. The clock showed that the contest would soon be finished. Suddenly, a bolt of lightning flashed and the power went out. After a moment it came back on — just in time for the clock to announce that the competition was over.

The judge asked the two contestants to reveal their finished software. Mohammed angrily said that he'd lost it all in the power outage. The judge turned to the other competitor. Jesus smiled and clicked a mouse, and a dazzling application appeared on his screen. After just a few moments, the judge was clearly impressed and declared Jesus the victor. When asked why the decision was made, the judge pointed out the unique characteristic that set the winner apart from all the other leaders: Jesus saves!

There is no other name by which we must be saved! All the rest of the best names, like Buddha, Mohammed, Joseph Smith, you name it, all have two things Jesus doesn't. One, a grave with a body in it. Second, rules on how to reach up to their standards. Salvation in Jesus is different from all other religions in the fact that there is no body of the Christ to be found. We don't worship at a shrine or honor a corpse. Jesus rose from the dead. No one else can document his or her leader's vitality now! Just as important, the stark difference between Christianity and all other religions is that their gods say, "Come up to my level and do certain things and I will accept you." Through Jesus, God came down to our level because we could never get up to his. No good deeds are necessary or even possible to get God's attention. All the other religions have the guru at the top of the mountain to whom one must climb and grovel! The Christian's God condescended to us!

And it's not the name Episcopalian or Lutheran or Catholic on our baptism certificate that will play a part in our salvation. Only the name Jesus. John Wesley once dreamed that he was at the gates of hell. He knocked and asked, "Are there any Roman Catholics here?" "Yes, many," was the reply. "Any Church of England men?" "Yes, many." "Any Presbyterians?" "Yes, many." "Any Wesleyans?" "Yes, many!" Disappointed and dismayed, especially at the last reply, he walked a little further in his dream and found himself at the gate of heaven. Here he repeated the same questions. "Any Wesleyans here?" "No," came the answer. "Whom do you have here then?" Wesley asked in astonishment. "We do not know of any here which you have named. The only name of which we know anything here is 'Christian.' "

Peter calls to 71 important people and to you and me: stop rejecting Jesus as the only way. This healed man you see is the result of an undeniable miracle. Jesus did it!

Must be saved: As if the source of salvation wouldn't have been enough of a stumbling block for proud Jews, Peter remains bold until the end, not by saying, "You can be saved," or "You may be saved," but you *must* be saved. To surrender to the Son is a divine necessity. All people must respond. Why? We all must respond because we are all like the lame man Peter healed, except that we are crippled spiritually. The crutch for spiritually lame people is the wooden cross where Jesus shed his blood.

The saving work has already been done. In Rotterdam, Holland, there was a home known as the House of 1,000 Terrors. It received its name during the sixteenth century, when the Protestant Dutch rose up against the Catholic King of Spain. A great army was sent to put down that rebellion. In captured Rotterdam, the Spaniards went from house to house searching out and killing citizens. One group was hiding in a house when they heard soldiers approaching. A thousand terrors gripped their hearts. Then a young man had an idea. He took a goat and killed it. With a broom he swept the blood under the doorway.

The soldiers reached the house and began to batter down the door. Noticing the blood coming out from under the door, one soldier said: "Come away, the work is already done here. Look at the blood." The people inside the house escaped.

The work of salvation is finished. But the work of the Spirit to let people know its reality still goes on. Jesus died for everyone — past, present, and future. But they don't know it yet. Will God write Scripture using your name today as you boldly live for Jesus? Put your name in the blank as I read the last verse of our text: Then, (   ), filled with the Holy Spirit, said to all, 'Salvation is found in no one else, for there is no other name under heaven given to men by which we must be saved.' "

Hear,
Hear

Acts 8:26-40

A woman went to see a divorce lawyer. Frantically she told him, "I must have a divorce from my husband immediately!" The lawyer asked, "Do you have any grounds?" "Yes, about five acres." "I mean, do you have a grudge?" the lawyer questioned. "No, just a carport."

Then the lawyer asked, "Does he beat you up?" "No," the woman replied, "I get up before he does." Exasperated, the attorney demanded, "Madam, why do you want a divorce from your husband?"

"Because it is impossible to communicate with that man!"

Question: How well do we hear God's voice? This text is a call to get the earwax out of our ears, perhaps to get a hearing aid, cup our hand over our ears at least, and listen intently to what God is saying!

It's a spectacular story with miracles galore. How did they happen? God was acting behind the scenes to make sure what he wanted done got done. First, God spoke to Philip and told him where to go. Next there was a pool of water on a dry, desert road right when they needed it. Third, Philip didn't get to rejoice with the new Christian because he was "energized" to another town immediately after the baptism.

Ah, but there was another miracle: how did Philip keep up with the chariot pulled by an animal? Perhaps he had Elijah-endurance so he could make a spiritual difference in the lonely man who was traveling on the super-highway of the day from Jerusalem to Egypt.

77

Who is this eunuch? He was probably an interesting fellow who may have been a proselyte who had been circumcised because he was tired of the loose morals and the many gods of the Gentiles and had found out that Judaism gave life meaning. Or this unnamed man did not proselytize, but attended Jewish synagogues and read Jewish Scripture. He was called a God-fearer.

We do know that the eunuch was an important and influential person who was a representative of the queen from the present country of Sudan. We know that he was hungry. He was hungry to learn about God, and he had questions.

When God unites a listening ear (Philip) and a hungry heart (the eunuch), God does even more miracles!

I see God's voice at least three times in this text. In verse 26, the angel tells Philip generally where to go. In verse 29, the Spirit says more specifically to Philip, who had his radar on high, what person to speak to. And in verses 32 and 35, the Holy Spirit is wooing the eunuch to faith in the Messiah.

How well do we listen to God? Do we hear his voice speaking to us through the Bible? Can we hear his nudges when we pray? Are we in tune with his Spirit enough to know when he is impressing something upon us — to stop, to go, to turn, to speak up? Do we hear God's voice in the godly advice from fellow Christians? Are we obedient to these directions from God?

What gives us dull ears? Why don't we hear as well as we should? Is it sinful wax or congenital hard of hearing? Or is it a combination of many things? Dr. Jesus is looking in your ears even as you hear these words and asking about what is causing your ear problems:

• Is it because you're too busy and don't take time to listen to his Love Letter?

• Is it because you are afraid you won't hear him right?

• Is it because you don't really know God, so how can you know his voice?

• Is it rebellion? You hear him, but you don't want to follow through?

• Are all the other voices in the world drowning out the voice of the One who loves you most?

On this fifth Sunday of Easter God is speaking to each of us about listening to him and letting him match us up with hungry, God-starved hearts. When we listen to his gentle urgings, we will find that there are many eunuchs in the world who know about Jesus, but don't know him personally. How can they unless someone explains to them? God will use you right where you are and help you and he together to tell the world about Jesus.

It was the seventh game of the 1962 World Series. The San Francisco Giants had a man on second base, which put him near New York Yankee second baseman Bobby Richardson. When the Yankees decided to change pitchers, Richardson, who was a Christian, saw a unique opportunity. While the new pitcher was warming up, he walked over to the man on second and asked him if he knew Jesus as his Savior.

When the runner reached the dugout later, he asked teammate Felipe Alou, who also was a Christian, what was going on. "Even in the seventh game of the World Series," he said to Felipe, "you people are still talking about Jesus." Like Philip, Bobby Richardson heard God's voice and responded.

Here is a true story that occurred a few years ago at the University of Southern California. There was a professor of philosophy there who was a deeply committed atheist. His primary goal for one required class was to spend the entire semester attempting to prove that God couldn't exist. His students were always afraid to argue with him because of his impeccable logic.

For twenty years he had taught this class and no one had ever had the courage to go against him. Some had argued in class at times, but no one had ever really challenged him. Nobody would speak against his belief because he had a reputation.

At the end of every semester, on the last day, he would say to his class of 300 students. "If there is anyone here who still believes in God, stand up!" In twenty years, no one had ever stood up. They knew what he was going to do next. He would continue, "Because anyone who does believe in God is a fool. If God existed, he could stop this piece of chalk from hitting the ground and breaking. Such a simple task to prove that he is God, and yet he can't do it." And every year he would drop the chalk onto the tile floor of the classroom and it would shatter into a hundred pieces. All of the students could do nothing but stop and stare. Most of the students were convinced that God couldn't exist. Certainly, a number of Christians had slipped through, but for twenty years, they had been too afraid to stand up.

Well, a few years ago, there was a freshman who happened to get enrolled in the class. He was a committed Christian and had heard stories about this professor. He had to take the class because it was one of the required classes for his major. And he was afraid. But for three months that semester, he prayed every morning that he would have the courage to stand up no matter what the professor said or what the class thought.

Finally the day came. The professor said, "If there is anyone here who still believes in God, stand up!" The professor and the class of 300 people looked at him, shocked, as he stood up at the back of the classroom. The professor shouted, "You fool! If God existed, he could keep this piece of chalk from breaking when it hit the ground!" He proceeded to drop the chalk, but as he did, it slipped out of his fingers, off his shirt cuff, onto the pleats of his pants, down his leg, and off his shoe. As it hit the ground, it simply rolled away, unbroken.

The professor's jaw dropped as he stared at the chalk. He looked up at the young man and then ran out of the lecture hall. The young man who had stood up proceeded to walk to the front of the room and share his faith in Jesus for the next half-hour. All the students stayed and listened as he told of God's love for them and of his power through Jesus!

I believe Philip and the eunuch give us God's plan in witnessing as we listen to the Spirit:

1. *Listen to what God says and act on it:* When God nudges you to speak to someone or go somewhere, do it! It's a process of learning to listen to the Spirit through the Word and in our spirit controlled by him. Listen and act even if it seems unlikely. The angel led Philip away from a hotbed of witness opportunities to a seemingly inappropriate place: a deserted road. God cares for a single convert,

no matter how hard or opposed to God he might be. When God says, "Go," go!

2. *Ask thought-provoking questions:* If you don't know what else to say, ask a meaningful, spiritual question or play off something they just said to ask a question related to it. All Philip asked was what God gave him, "Do you understand what you are reading?" I can guarantee that people are more ready to talk about spiritual things than we are ready to initiate it. Dr. Waylon Moore encourages us in witnessing "never to presuppose a negative response" in speaking to people about Jesus!

3. *Listen to them and then answer them with Jesus:* You don't have to have all the answers. Just listen and then tell them about what the Bible says about Jesus. "Then Philip began with that very passage of Scripture and told him the good news about Jesus." Philip hadn't had years of training or school; Christianity had just begun. But he knew and had experienced Jesus. So he listened and then testified. The eunuch knew God, but now he knew Jesus!

4. *Don't make it harder than it is:* Obviously Philip told him more specifics than we have recorded because the hungry eunuch knew enough to ask to be baptized. But he had faith and he wanted to fulfill God's wishes for him, so he asked to be baptized. "Why shouldn't I be baptized?" Yes, why not? God had done his job in giving faith. Let's not add any more than Scripture does to give people assurance of faith!

5. *Keep at it:* Philip had the privilege of baptizing a new Christian, but he didn't get to see the eunuch grow up spiritually. That's okay, Philip just kept on doing what God was calling him to do: "preaching the gospel in all the towns until he reached Caesarea." Don't give up. Every day ask God to help you find a eunuch!

Each morning as you put in your spiritual hearing aids, be sure you turn them loud enough to hear God say to you what he said to his Son at his baptism: "You are my beloved child. I love you and I am well pleased with you!" Ooh, I like that. Now I can take on the world for Jesus!

To Have And To Hold (Your Tongue)

Acts 10:44-48

There once was a Roman Catholic priest, an Episcopalian rector, a Presbyterian minister, and a Lutheran pastor who met together for lunch on a regular basis. One afternoon they got in a confessional mood and the minister suggested that they talk about their personal problems.

The priest confessed that he was a compulsive gambler. The rector admitted that he had an obsession about attractive women. The minister hesitated, but then admitted that he was an alcoholic. Then all three turned to the Lutheran pastor and asked him what his problem was. "Well," he confessed, "I'm a compulsive gossip, and I can't wait to get out of here!"

Last week the eunuch was a God-fearer who became a Christian. We meet another God-fearer today. Last week the eunuch said, "Why shouldn't I be baptized?" Today, on behalf of many people, another man says, "Can anyone keep these people from being baptized?" Last week we asked God to open our ears and speak to us. Today we ask God to use our tongues to lift up Jesus' name!

New ground was again being broken in the apostle's ministry. The apostle Peter had had a vision that told him to not be afraid to welcome believing Gentiles into the kingdom. At the same time (a day earlier), a God-fearing Gentile named Cornelius had an angelic visitor who told him to send for Peter and have him come to his home. A divine connection was being made in the heavens to bring about our text today. Cornelius obeyed the angel; Peter listened to God, and the entourage from Joppa met Cornelius and friends in Caesarea and Pentecost II happened!

"While he (Peter) was still speaking"(v. 44), the Holy Spirit came on all who heard the message. This was the same preacher God had used on Pentecost, and the Spirit had the same effect: speaking in tongues. But there is one major difference here: this visit by the Holy Spirit caused the faith birthday of these people. They became Christians that day and were baptized soon afterwards.

I wonder if Peter was surprised that all these Gentiles believed so readily. As a little aside to the main point of our text, are we astonished when people become Christians, especially unlikely candidates in our estimation of things? Maybe that is our problem. Our estimation is too low of what God can and wants to do. We don't expect enough from our great and faithful God.

Think about what the Trinity has done to effect the salvation of all who will only receive it. God desires all to be saved. The Holy Spirit's most important work and one that he does continually is wooing people to show them their sin and their Savior. Jesus accomplished the purchase from sin and the devil already, and no one can change that fact. No wonder people like football/baseball star Deion Sanders or the son of the famous atheist Madalyn Murray O'Hair have become Christians. We shouldn't be surprised. God never gives up. He keeps on knocking!

A nurse on the pediatric ward, before listening to the little ones' chests, would plug the stethoscope into their ears and let them listen to their own hearts. Their eyes would always light up with awe. But she never got a response equal to four-year-old David's. Gently she tucked the stethoscope in his ears and placed the disk over his heart. "Listen," she said, "what do you suppose that is?"

He drew his eyebrows together in a puzzled line and looked up as if lost in the mystery of the strange tap-tap-tapping in this chest. Then his face broke out in a wondrous grin. "Is that Jesus knocking?" he asked.

God never gives up. Neither should we!

But let's go back to our text. " And they spoke in tongues." Oh, no! One of those "supernatural gifts" that one part of

Christendom says is obsolete, while another says is active, a gift for today. One side is fearful of it; the other gladly gives it prominence. Were these tongues spoken at Cornelius's home ecstatic gibberish or was it a known tongue? We don't know. Let's not get caught in a debate over this gift. Let's simply ask: what is the purpose of the gift and what did this new household of Christians use their tongues for?

They used them to exalt Jesus. It was proof that they had been given faith in Jesus.

What about the use of our tongues today? When we became a Christian (at our baptism or at another faith birthday), we became a brand new creation. That includes your tongue. No one can *say* Jesus is Lord, except by the Holy Spirit. You must use your tongue to speak that wonderful truth! When we remember our baptism and how Jesus changed us there, our speech life is nourished.

How adept are we at using our tongues as the Acts 10 people did? "For they heard them speaking in tongues and *praising God!*" Do we continually praise God by what we say, by how we build up those made in the image of God, and by what we say behind the backs of those made in the image of God? Is your tongue a new creation each day or dangerous, like an old acidic, corrupt, and dead battery?

The story that began our message was about gossip. Has God brought a running tongue under the control of the Holy Spirit? Why do we say so much that is untrue and that damages reputations and churches and families? We rarely seem to think it's wrong. An unknown author has written this about the evil of the tongue:

> *I have no respect for justice. I maim without killing. I break hearts and ruin lives. I am cunning and malicious and gather strength with age. The more I am quoted, the more I am believed. I flourish at every level of society. My victims are helpless. They cannot protect themselves against me, for I have no face or no name. To track me down is impossible. The harder you try, the more elusive I become.*
>
> *I am nobody's friend. Once I tarnish a reputation, it is never quite the same. I topple governments and*

wreck marriages. I ruin careers, cause sleepless nights, heartaches, and grief. I make innocent people cry into their pillow. I make headlines and heartaches.

I am called gossip. The next time you want to tell a story about someone ... think. Is it true? Is it necessary? Is it kind? If not, please don't say it!

Your wayward tongue not only hurts others, but it will eventually hurt you, too. An elderly grandfather was growing deaf, so he decided to buy a hearing aid. Two weeks later he stopped at the store where he had bought it and told the manager he could now pick up conversation quite easily, even in the next room. "Your relatives must be happy to know that you can hear so much better," beamed the delighted storeowner. "Oh, I haven't told them yet," the man chuckled. "I've just been sitting around listening — and you know what? I changed my will twice!"

What about the jokes we tell? Is the light side, laughter-inducing part of our tongue under the lordship of Jesus? Here's a guideline to go by besides the Scriptural admonition of Ephesians 4:29: "Do not let any unwholesome talk come out of your mouths, but only what is helpful for building others up according to their needs, that it may benefit those who hear it."

It's a poor joke when ...
Some person blushes with embarrassment.
Some heart carries away an ache.
Something sacred is made to appear comical.
A person's weakness provides cause for laughter.
Profanity is required to make it funny.
Everyone can't join in the laughter.
A little child is brought to tears.

And what about criticism? Do you have a sharp tongue? Cornelius and his friends were given all of the Holy Spirit. We too have all of the Spirit through faith. But does the Holy Spirit have all of us, including our tongue? If you received a dime for kind words spoken about people and had to pay a nickel for the unkind ones, how rich or poor would you be? You can almost hear the gentle exasperation in James' voice as he mouths these words as the Holy Spirit writes through him: "With the tongue we praise our Lord and Father and with it we curse men, who have been made in God's likeness. Out of the same mouth come praise and cursing. My brothers, this should not be" (James 3:9-10).

Here is one example I predict all our families can relate to: How often do we, as Christians, at 10:45 a.m. on a Sunday morning, love Jesus, lift up his name, honor him, and speak Scripture, but 45 minutes later on the way home in the family van pick on and criticize each other? How can we sing Jesus' name over and over and pray for others one minute, and then backstab our sister or brother or use profanity directed at "that stupid driver" ahead of me the next?

Where's the hope for our speaking habits? First, we must learn and receive strength from Jesus, the One who kept his mouth shut and didn't even defend himself when accused at his trial. Our hope is in the cross and the open tomb of this Easter season and the One who conquered both. He forgives wayward tongues and empowers us always to speak the truth in love. The hope is hearing Jesus' tongue say, "Father, forgive them for they know not what they do," and using our tongues to cry out to him and say, "Forgive me, Jesus, and make me more like you!"

The second thing we need to do after admitting our need and receiving forgiveness is to be patient and let God refine the use of our tongues. It's a process to become more like Jesus. That's why the new creations in our text "asked Peter to stay with them for a few days." We're not finished products yet. We keep on learning and growing. Be patient and pray, "Lord, may the words of my mouth and the mediations of my heart be acceptable in your sight, O Lord, my Rock and my Redeemer!"

> *The tongue can be a blessing*
> *Or the tongue can be a curse;*
> *Say, friend, how are you using yours:*
> *For better or for worse?*

To Be Continued

Acts 1:1-11

Here is a remarkable story from World War II. From the island of Guam one of our mighty bombers took off for Kokura, Japan, with a deadly cargo. The sleek B-29 turned and circled above the cloud that covered the target for half an hour, then three-quarters of an hour, then 55 minutes, until the gas supply reached the danger point. It seemed a shame to be right over the primary target and then have to pass it up, but there was no choice. With one more look back, the crew headed for the secondary target. Upon arrival, they found the sky clear. They dropped the bomb and headed home.

Weeks later, an officer received information from military intelligence that chilled his heart. Thousands of Allied prisoners of war, the biggest concentrations of Americans in enemy hands, had been moved to Kokura a week before the intended bombing. The officer breathed, "Thank God for that cloud!"

The city that was hidden from the bomber was a prison camp and thousands of Americans are now alive who would have died if not for that cloud which rolled in from a sunlit sea. The secondary target that day was Nagasaki, and the missile intended for Kokura was the world's second atomic bomb!

We don't always understand why things happen, because God has higher purposes!

On this holy day when we celebrate the Ascension of Jesus we read a portion of a personal letter which Luke wrote to a man named Theophilus describing what Jesus had told the disciples in the forty days after he exited from the tomb. I can imagine confusion on the

89

disciples' face as they heard about "waiting for the gift" and "you will be baptized with the Holy Spirit" and "you will be witnesses to the ends of the earth." Did they know what he was talking about? I think they were especially consternated when, after Jesus headed heavenward, the angels talked about "he will come back."

All they knew was one thing: Jesus had left them without his physical presence anywhere. "Lord, we don't really care about the gift of the Holy Spirit or being witnesses right now. We want you." They stared into the sky and cried out, "Come, fix breakfast for us again, Lord! Master, show us one more miracle. We love your teaching, Jesus. Tell us some more. Please come back — we promise not to fight again." But Jesus wasn't to be seen visibly again.

The grieving disciples couldn't see God's higher purpose in leaving. Luke tells us that the Ascension is not about his going but his coming. Hey, disciples, wipe your tears, because in two ways he's not going, but coming!

First, unless Jesus left the Holy Spirit couldn't come: "When the Holy Spirit comes on you...." (v. 8). And second, unless Jesus left he couldn't come back someday in the future: I "will come back!" (v. 11). Not going, but coming! God had a higher purpose for leaving and he had to take something away to give something greater! Is that not just like God?

The physical Jesus could only be in one place at a time. His Spirit whom he sent can be everywhere at once. Through the ages. Across time zones. In every church at once. Jesus convicted the Sons of Boergenes when they asked for the places of honor in heaven and Peter when he tried to stop Jesus from dying, but the Holy Spirit can convict all sinners at one time.

Jesus comforted the woman caught in adultery after seeing her repentant heart, and he brought healing to Peter's mother-in-law by his presence and prayer, but the "greater gift," the Holy Spirit, comforts and encourages all his children and brings healing according to God's will to sick everywhere. Jesus imbued the disciples with boldness to go forth to witness, to cast out demons, and to declare the kingdom of God. Now the Holy Spirit does the same to all his disciples who name the name of Jesus.

Jesus went. The Spirit came. The Lord gives; the Lord takes; blessed be the name of the Lord!

But sometimes we just want Jesus back. It's not easy to see him go and trust in God's higher purpose. We're like the fly crawling on one of the great pillars of Saint Patrick's Cathedral in New York City. What does the fly know of the magnificent design of the church? All it sees is the little space of stone upon which it clings. The beautiful carvings and ornamental beauty are only like massive mountains impeding the fly's progress and obscuring his view.

We see only today and perhaps a glimpse of tomorrow. God sees the next day, the next week, the following month, and your whole life to come. During the Depression of the thirties a man lost his job, a fortune, a wife, and a home, but somehow he held onto his faith. That's all he had left. One day he stopped to watch some men building a stone church. One of them was chiseling a triangular piece of rock. The grieving man asked, "What are you going to do with that?" The workman said, "Do you see that little opening way up there near the spire? Well, I'm shaping this down here so that it will fit up there." The man started to cry as he walked away. God had spoken through the workman to show the man how he was working even in his terrible ordeal.

And it's from "way up there" that the second reason for Jesus' going will be fulfilled. Jesus will come back. After we have suffered down here a little while, we will know the eternal joys of heaven, which far outweigh the pains here. Jesus went to prepare a place for us. If he didn't go, what would our mansions look like? How would we ever truly appreciate heaven without living on this earth? And we can store up treasure in heaven while living here now.

The reason the disciples were discouraged as they stared into the sky is because they didn't understand the bigness of God or the fact of a higher purpose. They were wrong about the *future*, stuck in the *present* and depending on the *past*. And God wanted them focused on the comings!

When Jesus soared heavenward and they knew he wasn't coming back in a few minutes, all the earthly hopes and dreams of the disciples vanished. These Jewish men and all their countrymen had been under subjection to so many nations: the Babylonians, the Persians, the Greeks and now the Romans; and they all looked forward to the day when God would break into their world directly. Isn't that what Jesus' 33 years on the earth were about? Wait, Jesus, don't go. We thought that now that you have risen from the dead, we'd have a coming out party, an enthronement ceremony. You will be king and we all get to serve on your White Throne staff. Their future plans still included an earthly kingdom. God's higher purpose didn't!

They were also stuck in the present — only what their eyes could see *now!* Those mysterious rocket boosters on Jesus feet — they'd never seen those before. And the angels usually have good news for us. We don't like what we hear now. And hey, get that cloud out of the way; we want to see Jesus as long as we can. This time Jesus not only vanished (like many times before), but he also ascended, never to be seen by these men again on earth. The disciples were caught in a movie theatre that was showing a horror flick. The protagonist, the good guy, had just gotten in trouble and was killed. "Is he really dead — forever?" the movie watchers wonder. Or will he be supernaturally (and unrealistically) resurrected before the end of the movie? The eleven expected Jesus to come back immediately. He said he would and they only cared about their present condition!

And they were stuck in their knowledge of the past, too. The only people they knew of who had ever been bodily assumed into heaven were those two guys with names beginning with *E* in the Old Testament. Now Emmanuel also joined the elite group of Elijah and Enoch. What did it mean? Why did it happen again? They ran to check their Hebrew scrolls to get some answers. The past haunted these men.

What about us? Are we planning for a future we know nothing about? Are we stuck in the present and can't see past today by faith? Are we held back by what we learned in the past? Just as the coming of the Holy Spirit is invisible and the second coming of the Christ will be unknown until the trumpet sounds, so we can't understand, categorize, or even imagine the future God has for us

— even if we are going through what we consider "hell " right now. Our awesome God always has something better for us — especially when he takes something away.

There is a story in the Talmud about a wise and pious rabbi named Akiba. He took a trip to a strange country and took his three possessions with him: a donkey, a rooster, and a lamp. When he stopped at a village for lodging, the people drove him out and he was forced to spend the night in the forest. Being the holy man he was, he didn't complain and said, "All that God does is done well."

He found a tree under which to sleep, lit his lamp, and prepared to study the Torah before retiring. But a fierce wind blew out the light, forcing him to go to sleep early. Later that night, wild animals came through and chased away his rooster. Still later, thieves stole his donkey. But, in each case, Rabbi Akiba said, "All that God does is done well!"

The next morning he went back to the village. There he discovered that soldiers had killed everyone in the village. Had he been permitted to stay there, he too would have died. He learned also that the soldiers had traveled through the same part of the forest where he had slept. Had they seen the light of his lamp or heard his rooster crow or the donkey bray, again, he would have been killed. Thinking all these things, he replied as he always did: "All that God does is done well!"

Our text is the account of Jesus' last words on earth. That makes them immensely important. Jesus says to us today, "I might take, but I give still more. Things might go, but others will come. The Holy Spirit gives power to witness and I will escort my bride to heaven ... and that's a whole lot better than my staying!"

Decisions, Decisions

Acts 1:15-17, 21-26

Think of how many decisions you make in a day: What do I wear today? Should I take a different route to work due to construction? Should I have a bagel or an English muffin for breakfast? Should I talk with that person about yesterday or just blow it off? Which child is it that had flute lessons today? Should I get a quick twenty out at the ATM machine at lunch or after work? Do I need to pay bills today or can they wait until tomorrow? Do I have enough energy to run today or not? Should I drive to the corner gas station for milk or go all the way to Wal-Mart? Which sitcom should I watch tonight? Should I pick up the phone or let the machine get it?

Other decisions are harder and much more life impacting. Should we invest in a new car or not? Which one? Buy or lease? New or used? Is it time to put our child in a private school? Should we close in the garage or save the money for a vacation? Do I really want to join this church? Is this the woman God wants me to marry or am I just in lust? Should Grandpa live on his own or with us, or be put in a retirement home? Should I bail my troubled kid out of jail or show him tough love and make him learn that there are consequences for bad choices? Should I be buried or cremated?

Without outside help and guidance, decisions like these every day can be paralyzing. And what if the question and answer are not specifically condemned or approved in the Bible? What should be my reaction? What is God's will anyway? And why is it so hard to discern it sometimes?

95

Should we do what one man did? Desiring to know God's will, he decided to open the Bible randomly and blindly point to a verse. His finger landed on, "Whatever your hand finds to do, do it with all your might." "Good," he thought, "I'll try it again." This time he read: "Whatever you are about to do, do quickly!" "So far, so good. Okay, Lord, be a little more specific, please." He let the Bible flop open a third time, closed his eyes and pointed. The verse read: "And Judas went out and hanged himself."

Maybe some of you have done that before. I wouldn't suggest that. Rather I would suggest the path that Peter and the disciples took in our text for today. Soon after Jesus had returned to heaven and before he sent the Holy Spirit to guide, the apostles had a hard decision to make. A very important decision. A church-impacting choice. Who would be chosen as the replacement for Judas? Who would be put on the stained glass windows alongside Peter, James, and John? Who would probably be martyred for the sake of the gospel? No, most importantly, who would "become a witness with us of his resurrection" (v. 22)?

Judas was dead. Two names were put forward. The first was Joseph Barsabbas, who had the nickname Justus, and the other was Matthias. We don't know much about these godly men. Church father Eusebius says both were part of the seventy disciples Jesus had sent out earlier in his ministry. Papias says Barsabbas drank deadly poison, but did not die. Matthias is said to have preached and suffered martyrdom in Ethiopia. Not much more is known about these men.

We do know one had to be chosen above the other. According to what we know from history, the names of the candidates were written on stones and then the stones were placed in a vessel and the vessel was shaken until one fell out.

"Who will it be? Matthias on my right. Joseph on my left. Shake. Shake. Shake. Oh, there it goes. Who is it? When it stops rolling we will know. It's ... It's ... Matthias. Congratulations, brother!"

Don't you wish decisions were that easy? Have your own rocks with peel-off labels on them. Let's see: A Ford Explorer or a Nissan

Pathfinder? Dad goes to a rehab home or he lives with us. Oops. I don't like that answer. I'll do it again.

Don't suppose that Peter and Company took this lightly. Just like the use of the Thummim and Urim in the Old Testament, they knew that God had called them to decipher his will this way, and they knew that God controlled the roll of the stones that were placed in the vessel. God had chosen Matthias — no questions asked. No recounts needed. It wasn't luck or chance. It's not like the lottery when you pick a few numbers at random or the ping-pong balls lining up to a certain sequence of numbers by random chance. And the choice wasn't voted upon, therefore resting on human wisdom. I wonder if Joseph would have won by a human vote perhaps because he was better known or liked. God didn't choose that way. The heart of the king is in God's hand. So are the dice!

I wish that God owned a chain of airplane companies that fly advertising banners overhead. He could fly over my house each day and tell me, "Yes, private school is the way. And buy a casket, you cheapskate." It would be a whole lot easier!

Instead, God gives us, except for the dice, what the early disciples had — and more!

1. *Start with Scripture.* Peter did. Before this choosing process began, Peter stood up and quoted Scripture, thus knowing that what had happened to Judas was foretold and that they could take another step. If we knew the Bible better, we wouldn't be so stymied at times. No, perhaps the specifics you want are not there, but is there an overriding principle to follow? God, in his love, often brings Scripture to our remembrances, but we need to know them first. God uses the Bible preeminently, but he also chooses to use circumstances to help guide us, too. He's in charge of these circumstances and thus uses them to fulfill his plan. Some would call them "closed and open doors." Remember, when God closes one door, look for another — or for a window. God also shows us his will by the counsel of godly, Christian friends. Ask their opinions. Maybe they will know a biblical principle to follow. But be sure your friends are really faithful friends who won't just tell you what you want to hear. And finally, God loves to hear his

children pray and often gives impression or nudges to us as we seek him. God wants his children to know his will!

2. *God knows your heart!* Verse 24 says, "Then they prayed, 'Lord, you know everyone's heart. Show us who of these two you have chosen.'" God knows everyone's heart. That can be good or bad depending on what is in your heart. You can't hide your real motive and you can't bamboozle God. So we can just be honest. And that's good, especially when we really are stumped and must step out with what we think is the best decision. Guess what? You can't go wrong if your heart is right. God sees it and he will turn even a less-than-perfect decision into good because he knows you were seeking him. "The Lord does not look at the things man looks at. Man looks at the outward appearance, but the Lord looks at the heart" (1 Samuel 16:7).

3. *God's will is always to be a witness.* God's will is always what the apostles prayed for in verse 22: "Which one of these will become a witness with us of his resurrection?" Is this God's concern in all things? Yes. But how can the decision between closing up the garage or going on a cruise be directly related to sharing our faith and bringing others to Christ? Will working outside intensely give you more opportunities to witness to your neighbors? Will there be contractors involved who will see Jesus in you? Is the vacation needed so you can stop from being burned out at work and thus have more strength to be who God has called you to be? Are you willing to share Jesus with your dinner companions on the ship? Here are a couple questions to ask yourself as you make a decision: Will this choice lift up the risen Christ more? Will it help me in my Christian life and faith? Will it send us forth into the harvest field boldly?

These suggestions depend on the one thing Peter and the gang didn't have to help guide them, at least not in the way we do: the Holy Spirit. Pentecost had not yet happened. That's why we don't use dice or rocks anymore. All those practices ceased because the Holy Spirit resides in us and speaks to us through the Word and godly counsel, reads our heart well (he lives there!), and uses us to carry the message of the gospel in all we do.

Does God care about every decision? Should we pray about each one? Well, as you stand in front of your hanging clothes in your closet, though he does care about how you look, don't expect him to guide your hand to the dress of the day or the perfectly coordinated tie. And sometimes we paralyze ourselves and wait for an answer when common sense says, "Do it! You must!" There are simply some things we as Christians are called to do, and we can't use prayer as an excuse to put it off.

Communion with the Christ each day ("pray without ceasing") helps us know and clears the way. Setting our minds on things above helps us to sense automatically God's leading often times. He can give a check in your spirit and uneasiness or peace that passes understanding.

God wants you to know his will. He forgives freely those who repent after making a bad choice. And he even graciously brings good out of evil for his children who love and follow him! Count on it!

Books In This Cycle B Series

GOSPEL SET
A God For This World
Sermons for Advent/Christmas/Epiphany
Maurice A. Fetty

The Culture Of Disbelief
Sermons For Lent/Easter
Donna E. Schaper

The Advocate
Sermons For Sundays After Pentecost (First Third)
Ron Lavin

Surviving In A Cordless World
Sermons For Sundays After Pentecost (Middle Third)
Lawrence H. Craig

Against The Grain — Words For A Politically Incorrect Church
Sermons For Sundays After Pentecost (Last Third)
Steven E. Albertin

FIRST LESSON SET
Defining Moments
Sermons For Advent/Christmas/Epiphany
William L. Self

From This Day Forward
Sermons For Lent/Easter
Paul W. Kummer

Out From The Ordinary
Sermons For Sundays After Pentecost (First Third)
Gary L. Carver

Wearing The Wind
Sermons For Sundays After Pentecost (Middle Third)
Stephen M. Crotts

Out Of The Whirlwind
Sermons For Sundays After Pentecost (Last Third)
John A. Stroman

SECOND LESSON SET
Humming Till The Music Returns
Sermons For Advent/Christmas/Epiphany
Wayne Brouwer

Ashes To Ascension
Sermons For Lent/Easter
John A. Stroman